A **FALCON** GUIDE ®

Walking
Raleigh/Durham

Rebecca C. Mann

 Endorsed by the American Volkssport Association

D1173403

FALCON®

GUILFORD, CONNECTICUT
An imprint of The Globe Pequot Press

To Pete, with love—Write on

A FALCON GUIDE ®

Cover photo: Steve Dunwell Photography, Inc./Index
Stock
Maps: Tony Moore/Moore Creative Designs
All photos are by the author unless otherwise noted.

Library of Congress Cataloging-in-Publication Data is
available.

ISBN 1-56044-1132-9

Manufactured in the United States of America
First Edition/First Printing

Contents

The Walks

Acknowledgments

This book would not have the pictures, maps, and information that it does were it not for some helpful people in Raleigh and Durham.

I am indebted to the local walking club, the Triangle Trailblazers, for sharing information about their walks in these cities.

Special thanks to Reyn Bowman and Edmund Purdy of the Durham Convention and Visitors Bureau, to Betty Baker at the Capital Area Visitor Center, and to David Heinl, Rebecca Moore, Shirley Tucker, and Nicole Galbo at the Greater Raleigh Convention and Visitors Bureau. I particularly appreciate Rebecca Moore's time, enthusiasm, and expertise. All these people took time to answer questions and provide the materials I needed.

Roxan and Vernon Daughtridge were kind enough to put me up as well as put up with me. Thanks to you both, and thanks to Wesley Daughtridge for the information about North Carolina State University.

I am also grateful to the staffs of Raleigh's and Durham's parks and recreation departments, Beth Timson at the Durham City/County Planning Department, the staffs of the Sheraton Raleigh Capital Center Hotel and the Durham Hilton, and to Jim and Sarah Lofton, hosts at the William Thomas House Bed and Breakfast. Wendy Weiher, Office of Duke Forest; Dr. William Louis Culberson at Duke Gardens; Sandy Roberts, at UNC–Chapel Hill Visitor Center; N. Jill Coleman at North Carolina State University; and Janet Atwood, librarian at Wilkes Community College made the work easier and more productive. Thanks to Theresa Stewart at the Wilkes Chamber of Commerce for her helpful suggestions at the beginning of my research.

I am grateful for the assistance provided by the editors of this series, Judith Galas and Cindy West. Judith's replies to my questions were always prompt and helpful.

Finally, thanks to my husband, Pete, for everything: walking in the heat of summer to help measure the walks, invaluable editing assistance, and most of all, listening and responding to me throughout the process.

Duke Chapel is the focus and best-known symbol of Duke University. (Courtesy North Carolina Collection/University of North Carolina Library at Chapel Hill)

Foreword

For more than 20 years, Falcon has guided millions of people to America's wild outside, showing them where to paddle, hike bike, bird, fish, climb, and drive. With this walking series, we at Falcon ask you to try something just as adventurous. We invite you to experience this country from its sidewalks, not its back roads, and to stroll through some of America's most interesting cities.

In their haste to get where they are going, travelers often bypass this country's cities, and in the process, they miss the historic and scenic treasures hidden among the bricks. Many people seek spectacular scenery and beautiful settings on top of the mountains, along the rivers, and in the woods. While nothing can replace the serenity and inspiration of America's natural wonders, we should not overlook the beauty of the urban landscape.

The steel and glass of municipal mountains reflect the sunlight and make people feel small in the shadows. Birds sing in city parks, water burbles in the fountains, and along the sidewalks walkers can still see abundant wildlife— their fellow human beings.

Falcon's many outdoor guidebooks have encouraged people not only to explore and enjoy America's natural beauty but to also preserve and protect it. Our cites are equally meant to be enjoyed and explored and their irreplaceable treasures need care and protection.

When travelers and walkers want to explore something that is inspirational and beautiful, we hope they will lace up their walking shoes and point their feet toward one of this country's many cities. For there, along the walkways, they are sure to discover the excitement, history, beauty, and charm of urban America.

—*The Editors*

Map Legend

Walk Route		Picnic Area		
Interstate Highways		River or Stream		
Streets and Roads		Lake or Pond		
Path	= = = =	Interstate	(40)	
Start/Finish of Loop Walk	S/F	U.S. Highway	(15)	
Parking Area	P	State and County Roads	(54)	
Building		Railroad	++++++++	
Church or Cathedral	†	Bus Stop	B	
Restrooms, Male and Female	👫	Steps		
Accessible Facility/Trail	♿	Map Orientation	N	
		Scale of Distance	0 0.5 1 Miles	

Raleigh Overview Map

10 Blue Jay Point County Park

Alexander Dr
US 70

Glenwood Ave

To Henderson
US 1

Six Forks Rd

Raleigh/Durham International Airport

Umstead State Park

I-40

Blue Ridge Rd

Shelley Lake

9

Millbrook Rd

I-440

To Rocky Mount

7

Wade Ave

Hillsborough St

3

4 N.C. Capitol

New Bern Ave

64 264

6 NCSU

5

2

1

M.L.K. Jr. Blvd

64

Lake Johnson

8

Pullen Park

I-440

RALEIGH

US 1

I-40

To Wilmington

N

0   2.5   5
Miles

Durham/Chapel Hill Overview Map

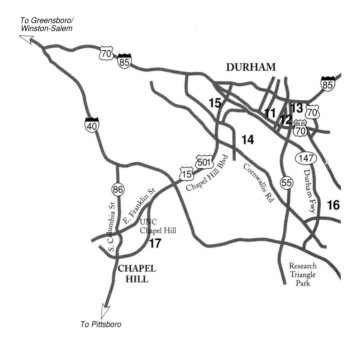

To Greensboro/
Winston-Salem

70 85

DURHAM

85

15

11 13
12

70

BUS
70

14

147

501

15

Chapel Hill Blvd

Cornwallis Rd

55

Durham Fwy

16

40

86

S. Columbia St

E. Franklin St

UNC
Chapel Hill

17

CHAPEL
HILL

Research
Triangle
Park

To Pittsboro

N

0   2.5   5
Miles

Preface: Come Walk the Triangle

The cities that make up the region of North Carolina known as the Triangle offer miles of walking paths and hiking trails for exploring this area on foot. Each city has unique offerings for those who want to do more than drive through.

In Raleigh you can stroll down the streets of Oakwood and Blount historic districts, two areas that showcase some of the finest turn-of-the-century homes in this region. You can enjoy the museums of the capital city and the seats of government. Walk on the famous redbrick paths of the campus of North Carolina State University and see some of the famous sights of this large urban campus. Experience one of the premier greenways in the nation, the Capital Area Greenway. Although many of the trails in the greenway system are within city limits, you will enjoy wildlife, stands of pine, and even lakes and streams on some trails.

In Durham you will be awed by the sight of Duke Chapel and the grounds and buildings of Duke University. If you are a baseball fan, you will want to see two baseball fields: the old and the new homes of the Durham Bulls. Walk downtown and enjoy the architecture and charm of a Southern city claiming a vibrant past and a vigorous future.

Alumni and friends of the University of North Carolina at Chapel Hill, wherever they are, want to visit and revisit the lovely campus and the small town of Chapel Hill. Stroll down Franklin Street and recapture, or experience for the first time, the street's ambience and the campus that borders it. Learn for yourself why thousands of alumni and friends of the university are loyal Tar Heels and even nostalgic when they visit the campus's famous landmarks, such as the Old Well or Old East.

Walkers will be especially interested in knowing that the system of trails established in Raleigh in the mid-1970s allowed Raleigh to be named the first Green Survival City in the country in 1975. Sports fans everywhere are familiar with the Wolfpack of North Carolina State University, the Tar Heels of the University of North Carolina at Chapel Hill, and the Duke Blue Devils. These teams are legendary worldwide, and walks in this book will let you stroll by the homes of these famous teams.

If you are one of the many business people visiting the Triangle for a day, a week, or longer, use *Walking Raleigh/Durham* to help you unwind after a day of meetings and to learn more about the sights, history, and culture of the area. If a vacation has brought you here, these walks will give you a sampling of the many things to do and see. If you are a native of one of the three cities or the growing metropolitan area surrounding the cities, *Walking Raleigh/Durham* will introduce you to new sights and may inspire you to do some additional exploring in your own backyard. From the university campuses to the walks around the lakes to Research Triangle Park itself, business travelers, tourists, and residents will all find an appealing variety of walks to enable them to enjoy walking Raleigh and Durham.

How to Use this Guide

Walking the streets and boulevards of a city can take you into its heart and give you a feel for its pulse and personality. From the sidewalk looking up, you can appreciate its architecture. From the sidewalk peeking in, you can find the quaint shops, local museums, and great eateries that give a city its charm and personality. From its nature paths, you can smell the flowers, glimpse the wildlife, gaze at a lake, or hear a creek gurgle. Only by walking can you get close enough to read the historical plaques and watch the people. When you walk a city, you get it all—adventure, scenery, local color, good exercise, and fun.

We have designed this book so that you can easily find the walks that match your interests, time, and energy level. The Trip Planner is the first place you should look when deciding on a walk. This table will give you the basic information—a walk's distance, the estimated walking time, and the difficulty. The pictures or icons in the table also tell you specific things about the walk:

Every walk has something of interest, but this icon tells you that the route will have particular appeal to the shutterbug. So bring your camera. You will have great views of the city or the surrounding area, and you are likely to get some wonderful scenic shots.

Somewhere along the route you will have the chance to get food or a beverage. You will have to glance through the walk description to determine where and what kind of food and beverages are available. Walks that do not have the food icon probably are along nature trails or in noncommercial areas of the city.

During your walk, you will have the chance to shop. More detailed descriptions of the types of stores you will find can be found in the actual walk description.

This walk features something kids will enjoy seeing or doing—a park, zoo, museum, or play equipment. In most cases the walks that carry this icon are short and follow an easy, fairly level path. You know your young walking companions best. If your children are patient walkers who do not tire easily, then feel free to choose walks that are longer and harder. In fact, depending on a child's age and energy, most children can do any of the walks in this book. The icon only notes those walks we think they will especially enjoy.

Your path will take you primarily through urban areas. Buildings, small city parks, and paved paths are what you will see and pass.

You will pass through a large park or walk in a natural setting where you can see and enjoy nature.

The wheelchair icon means that the path is fully accessible. This walk would be easy for someone pushing a wheelchair or stroller. We have made every attempt to follow a high standard for accessibility. The icon means there are curb cuts or ramps along the entire route, plus a wheelchair-accessible bathroom somewhere along the way. The path is mostly or entirely paved, and ramps and unpaved surfaces are clearly described. If you use a wheelchair and have the ability to negotiate curbs and dirt paths or to wheel for longer distances and on uneven surfaces, you may want to skim the directions for the walks that do not carry this symbol. You may find other walks you will enjoy. If in doubt, read the full text of the walk or call the contact source for guidance.

At the start of each walk description, you will find spe-

Picturesque Franklin Street is a popular shopping location for visitors to Chapel Hill.

cific information describing the route and what you can expect on your walk.

General location: Here you will get the walk's general location in the city or within a specific area.

Special attractions: Look here to find the specific things you will pass. If this walk has museums, historic homes, restaurants, or wildlife, it will be noted here.

Difficulty: For this book we have selected walking routes that an average person in reasonable health can complete easily. In most cases, you will be walking on flat surfaces with few, if any, hills. Your path will most likely be a maintained surface of concrete, asphalt, wood or packed dirt. It will be easy to follow, and you will be only a block or so from a phone, other people or businesses. If the walk is less than a mile, you may be able to walk comfortably in street shoes. If you are in doubt about whether you can manage a particular walk, read the description carefully or call the listed contact for more information.

Distance and estimated time: This gives the total distance of the walk. The time allotted for each walk is based on walking time only, which we have calculated at about thirty minutes per mile, a slow pace. Most people have no trouble walking a mile in half an hour, and people with some walking experience often walk a twenty-minute mile. If the walk includes museums, shops, or restaurants, you may want to add sightseeing time to the estimate.

Services: Here you will find out if such things as restrooms, parking, refreshments, or information center are available and where you are likely to find them.

Restrictions: The most often noted restriction is pets, which almost always have to be leashed in a city. Most cities also have strict "pooper-scooper" laws, and they enforce them. But restrictions may also include the hours or days a museum or business is open, age requirements, or whether you can ride a bike on the path. If there is something you cannot do on this walk, it will be noted here.

For more information: Each walk includes at least one contact source for you to call for more information. If an agency or business is named as a contact, you will find its phone number and address in Appendix B. This appendix also includes contact information for any business or agency mentioned anywhere in the book.

Getting started: Here you will find specific directions to the starting point. Most walks are closed loops, which means they begin and end at the same point. Thus, you do not have to worry about finding your car when your walk is over.

If a walk is not a closed loop, this section will tell you where the walk ends, and you will find the exact directions back to your starting point at the end of the walk's directions.

Some downtown walks can be started at any one of several hotels the walk passes. The directions will be for the main starting point, but this section will tell you if it is possible to pick up the walk at other locations. If you are staying at a downtown hotel, it is likely that a walk passes in front of or near your hotel's entrance.

Public transportation: Many cities have excellent transportation systems; others have limited services. If it is possible to take a bus or commuter train to the walk's starting point, you will find the bus or train noted here. You may also find some information about where the bus or train stops.

Overview: Every part of a city has a story. Here is where you will find the story or stories about the people, neighborhoods, and history connected to your walk.

The Walk

When you reach this point, you are ready to start walking. In this section you will not only find specific and detailed directions, but also learn more about the things you are passing. Those who want only the directions and none of the extras can find the straightforward directions by looking for the ➤.

What to wear

The best advice is to wear something comfortable. Leave behind anything that binds, pinches, rides up, falls down, slips off the shoulder, or comes undone. Otherwise, let common sense, the weather, and your own body tell you what to wear.

What to take

Be sure to take water. Strap a bottle to your fanny pack or tuck a small one in a pocket. If you are walking several miles with a dog, remember to take a small bowl so your pet can have a drink, too.

Carry some water even if you will be walking where refreshments are available. Several small sips taken throughout a walk are more effective than one large drink at the walk's end. Avoid drinks with caffeine or alcohol because they deplete rather than replenish your body's fluids.

Safety and street savvy

Mention a big city and many people immediately think of safety. Is it safe to walk there during the day? What about at night? Are there areas I should avoid?

You should use common sense whether you are walking in a small town or a big city, but safety does not have to be your overriding concern. American cities are enjoyable places, and you will find that they are generally safe places.

Any safety mishap in a large city is likely to involve petty theft or vandalism. So, the biggest tip is simple: Do not tempt thieves. Purses dangling on shoulder straps or slung over your arm, wallets peeking out of pockets, arms burdened with packages, valuables on the car seat—all attract the pickpocket, purse snatcher, or thief. If you look like you could easily be relieved of your possessions, you may be.

Do not carry a purse. Put your money in a money belt or tuck your wallet into a deep side pocket or your pants or skirt or in a fanny pack that rides over your hip or stomach. Lock your valuables in the trunk of your car before you park and leave for your walk. Protect your camera by wearing the strap across your chest, not just over your shoulder. Better yet, put your camera in a backpack.

You also will feel safer if you remember the following:

- Be aware of your surroundings and the people near you.

- Avoid parks or other isolated places at night.

- Walk with others.

- Walk in well-lit and well-traveled areas.

The walks in this book were selected by people who had safety in mind. No walk will take you through a bad neighborhood or into an area of the city that is known to be dangerous. So relax and enjoy your walk.

the walks

Walk name	Difficulty	Distance (miles)	Time	🎡	🏭	🌳	💐	📖	🔍	📷
Downtown Raleigh										
1 City Scenes	easy	1.3 miles	45 minutes	✓	✓		✓	✓	✓	✓
2 Capitol Walk	easy	1.5 miles	45 minutes	✓	✓		✓	✓	✓	✓
3 Government and Museums	easy	1.3 miles	45 minutes	✓	✓		✓	✓	✓	✓
4 Historic Neighborhoods	easy	1.5 miles	45 minutes		✓			✓	✓	
5 Gardens and Shopping	easy	6.25 miles	3.25 hours		✓	✓		✓	✓	
North Carolina State University										
6 Wolfpack Walk	easy	2 miles	1 hour	✓	✓	✓		✓	✓	✓
7 JC Raulston Arboretum	easy	0.5 mile	30 minutes	✓		✓				
Greater Raleigh										
8 Lake Johnson Trail	moderate	3.5 miles	2 hours			✓	✓	✓		✓
9 Shelley Lake Trail	easy	2.25 miles	1.25 hours			✓	✓		✓	✓
10 Blue Jay Point Nature Walk	easy	0.75 mile	30 minutes			✓	✓	✓		✓

Downtown Durham

	Wheelchair access	Distance	Time	City setting	Nature setting	Good for kids	Shopping	Food	Bring Camera
11 City Sights	easy	0.8 mile	30 minutes			✓		✓	✓
12 Campus and Shopping	easy	2.8 miles	2.5 hours			✓	✓	✓	✓
13 Bull Durham	easy	2 miles	1 hour			✓	✓	✓	✓

Duke University

	Wheelchair access	Distance	Time	City setting	Nature setting	Good for kids	Shopping	Food	Bring Camera
14 Duke Chapel and Duke Gardens	easy	1.5 miles	45 minutes			✓	✓	✓	✓
15 Duke Forest	moderate	3.7 miles	2 hours		✓		✓	✓	

Greater Durham

	Wheelchair access	Distance	Time	City setting	Nature setting	Good for kids	Shopping	Food	Bring Camera
16 Research Triangle Park	moderate	6.5 miles	3.5 hour		✓		✓	✓	✓

Chapel Hill

	Wheelchair access	Distance	Time	City setting	Nature setting	Good for kids	Shopping	Food	Bring Camera
17 Tar Heels and Franklin Street	easy	4 miles	2 hours			✓	✓	✓	✓

the icons

Wheelchair access	City setting	Nature setting	Good for kids	Shopping	Food	Bring Camera

Meet Raleigh

General

County: Wake

Area code: 919

Size

286,834 people

88.1 square miles

Major highways

Interstates: I–85, I–40

U.S. highways: US 1, 64, 70, 401

State highways: NC 50, 54, 55, 97

Airport service

Air Canada, AirTran, American, Continental, Delta, Delta Express, Midway, Midwest Express, Northwest, Southwest, TWA, United, and US Airways

Recreation

Golf courses: 18 (5 public; 13 semiprivate)

Parks: 156 city and county parks covering 4,300 acres

Major industries

Government, education, research, healthcare, computers, electronics

Media

Television stations

ABC—Channel 11

CBS—Channel 5

Fox—Channel 22

NBC—Channel 17

PBS—Channel 4

UPN—Channel 28

Radio stations
  WPTF 680 AM—News radio, talk
  WUNC 91.5—National Public Radio member

Newspaper
  The News & Observer, morning daily

Special annual events
  Call the Greater Raleigh Convention and Visitors Bureau (919) 834–5000 or (800) 849–8499 to confirm dates and times for area events.

- February: Home and Garden Show

- April: Great Raleigh Road Race, Southern Women's Show, Civil War Living History

- May: Artsplosure

- July: July 4th celebration at North Carolina State Fairgrounds

- August: BuGFest!

- October: International Festival, Raleigh Jaycees Haunted House

- November: Raleigh Christmas Parade

- December: Christmas at Mordecai Historic Park, Executive Mansion Holiday Open House, Messiah "Sing-in," State Capitol Tree Lighting Celebration, Historic Oakwood Candlelight Tour, First Night Raleigh

Meet Durham

General

    County: Durham

    Area Code: 919

Size

    223,314 people

    299 square miles

Major highways

    Interstates: I–85, I–40

    U.S. highways: US 70, 15/501

    State highways: NC 54, 98, 147, 157, 751

Airport service

    Air Canada, AirTran, American, Continental, Delta, Delta Express, Midway, Midwest Express, Northwest, Southwest, TWA, United, and US Airways

Recreation

    Golf courses: 11 (7 public)

    Parks: More than 60 parks totaling 1,690 acres

Major industries

    Medicine, telecommunications, education, research

Media

    Television stations

        PBS—Channel 4

    Radio stations

        WDNC 620 AM—News, talk radio, sports

        WUNC 91.5 FM—National Public Radio member

Newspaper

    The Herald-Sun, morning daily

Special annual events

    For additional information, call (800) 722–BULL

- January–April: International Jazz Festival
- February: Native American Powwow
- April: DoubleTake Film Festival, Bennett Place Civil War Surrender Reenactment
- May: Bimbé Cultural Festival, Duke Children's Classic
- June: Edible Arts, Brightleaf Music Workshop and Finale
- June–July: American Dance Festival
- July: Festival for the Eno, Duke Homestead Tobacco Harvest Festival
- August: Duke Homestead Herb Day
- September: Bull Durham Blues Festival, Center-Fest
- November: Annual Juried Art Show
- December: Light-up Durham

In the Know

Weather

Raleigh and Durham are located in the piedmont of North Carolina along the western edge of the coastal plain, enabling the cities to enjoy temperate climates year-around. The cities enjoy four seasons; winters are rarely extreme.

July, with an average daily high temperature of 88° F, is the warmest month. January, with an average daily high temperature of 50° F, is the coldest. May through September are the warmest; July and August can be hot and humid (even the nights can be quite warm during those months with an average low in August of 66° F). Light clothing is all that is necessary in the summer months.

Winter months offer a variety of weather, ranging from brief cold periods with occasional light snow to rainy periods and sunny days. However, because of the temperate climate, sunny, pleasant days can be expected, even in the coldest months. Nights can be cold; the average low in December, January, and February is 31° F. You will need a variety of clothing for the winter months: a heavy coat for cold, damp winter evenings and layers of clothing for warm, sunny days that sometimes reach into the seventies even in January.

Transportation

By car: In Raleigh the main north–south routes are US 1 and US 401. On the northeast side of the downtown area, US 401 is Louisburg Road until it reaches the beltline, where it becomes Capital Boulevard; south of downtown, it is South Saunders Street.

The major east–west routes are I–40, US 64, US 1, and US 70. I–40 runs east–west, but becomes I–440, a beltline around the downtown area. In the southern part of the beltline, US 64 runs concurrently with I–40 and I–440. On the southeast corner of the beltline, I–40 goes east and the beltline is I–440/US 64. At Louisburg Road, US 1 merges with the beltline.

In Durham, the major north–south roads are US 15/501 and NC 55. In town, US 15/501 is Mangum Street going south one way and one-way Roxboro Street going north. NC 55 is also known as Alston Avenue.

The major east–west route is I–85. Other important east–west routes are US 70, which is Morgan Street west of downtown and Holloway Street east of downtown. The fastest way through town using an east–west route, however, is the Durham Freeway, NC 147, which connects I–85 to I–40 south of Durham in Research Triangle Park.

Names and numbers of streets and roads can sometimes change on what appears to be the same road. Roads may be referred to by a number, a name, and by a memorial name, which is confusing at times.

Metered parking, parking lots, and parking garages are available in the downtown areas of Raleigh and Durham.

By bus: Raleigh's Capital Area Transit (CAT) serves Raleigh with connections to Durham, Research Triangle, and Chapel Hill via the Triangle Transit Authority (TTA). You can also get connections with North Carolina State University's Wolfline and Amtrak. Most buses run from 5:30 A.M. to 11:00 P.M. Monday through Saturday. Exact fare is required or you can purchase an eleven-ride Ticketbook or a monthly pass, with unlimited rides.

Durham Area Transit Authority (DATA) serves the city of Durham and the Research Triangle with connections to Raleigh and Chapel Hill via the Triangle Transit Authority (TTA). Buses run from 5:30 A.M. to 11:30 P.M. Monday through Saturday. Exact fare is required or you can buy a twenty-ride DATA card or a monthly pass with unlimited rides. DATA buses accommodate wheelchair users and those with walkers and canes. Call DATA (919–683–DATA) or TTA at (919–549–9999) to confirm routes and schedules.

By air: Raleigh/Durham International Airport is located off I–40 between Durham and Raleigh near the Research Triangle Park. Several major airlines offer daily flights. Taxi service from the airport to downtown Raleigh costs about $23. The airport phone number is (919) 840–2123.

By train: Amtrak has daily service to and from Raleigh. Capital Area Transit in Raleigh has connections from the Moore Square Transit Station to the Amtrak station at 320 Cabarrus Street Monday through Saturday. CAT service is not available on Sunday.

Safety

Raleigh, Durham, and Chapel Hill are among some of the safest cities in the Southeast. Crime rates have gone down over the past few years, and these cities are proud of that. Follow basic precautions as you walk in and around the Triangle.

One crime that has increased over the past few years in this area is car theft. Always lock your car when you leave it. It is a good idea to store valuables out of sight in trunks or glove compartments rather than leaving them visible on car seats.

Greenways are safer to walk during daylight hours, and the Raleigh Department Parks and Recreation recommends that you do that. Also, during daylight hours it is easier to watch for uneven sidewalk and street surfaces and to read maps. Portions of some walks, particularly those on greenways, do not have streetlights. However, if you want to walk in the late evening or at night, you will probably have the company of fellow walkers on the warmer evenings of spring and fall, especially if you walk in the well-lit areas that are busy with tourists and in those that sponsor night activities, such as the City Market in Raleigh. A late-evening walk through the Sarah P. Duke Gardens at Duke University can be delightful, but stay in well-lighted areas.

You should also take some precautions to protect your health. If you are walking in the summer months in the

Triangle region, the combination of heat and humidity can, on rare occasions, create unsafe walking conditions, particularly if you have asthma or other breathing problems. Radio, newspaper, and television media publish heat indexes—a measure of the temperature based on the combination of heat and humidity. On particularly hot summer days, listen to these forecasts and make a decision about whether you think it is safe to walk, given the particular conditions of the day and the status of your health. Forecasters also warn when the ozone level is high, another danger for those with breathing problems.

The South is a popular place for certain insects, some of which can be an annoyance and some of which can be dangerous. Mosquitoes can be pesky, particularly during late summer in low-lying or damp areas. Wear mosquito repellent or carry it to use as needed on walks such as the Gardner Street Greenway in the Gardens and Shopping walk.

A more dangerous risk in the warm months is ticks. Not every tick carries disease; however, some can be carriers of Lyme disease and a potentially dangerous disease called Rocky Mountain spotted fever. Check your body and your head for ticks after your walk if you walk in late spring or summer. Ticks are only a potential problem in wooded areas. You should not worry about ticks on streets or sidewalks, and be assured that the walker who encounters a tick will be the exception rather than the rule.

To protect yourself from sunburn and dehydration in the warmer months, wear sunblock and carry water, particularly on longer walks.

The Story of the Triangle

The three cities of Raleigh, Durham, and Chapel Hill comprise an area known as the Triangle. The area gets its name from the three cities that form a triangle and from the three universities that anchor the points of the triangle. In the middle of this century, Research Triangle Park was created, which cemented the region's nickname.

However, early history in the region is the story of three separate cities that grew independent of each other while simultaneously playing important parts in state and national history.

The first Europeans to arrive in the area in the 1700s were Scots, Irish, and British, and they encountered several tribes of Native Americans, including the Eno, the Tuscarora, and the Occoneechi. Most of these were farming tribes, and they had settled in the area near the rivers, the Eno, the Flat, and the Little, which served as transportation and as food sources. These native peoples lived on the Great Indian Trading Path, a fur trading route, which eventually brought white traders to the area.

North Carolina was divided into the east and the west during the Revolutionary War. The western regions felt they suffered from excessive taxes levied on them by the colonial government in the eastern areas. The westerners, embittered by the high tax rates, formed an association called the Regulators, whose purpose was to obtain reforms. Their refusal to pay taxes finally led to the Battle of Alamance in 1771, when they were crushed by Gov. William Tryon. Inhabitants of the area around Raleigh, Chapel Hill, and what later became Durham were involved in these insurrections and helped to subdue the rebellion.

By the mid-1700s, the state's leaders were looking for a location for the seat of government. Many of the newly formed communities were contending for the honor; however, the present location of Raleigh was eventually chosen in 1792 because of its central location in the state, and, according to popular legend, because it was close to Isaac Hunter's Tavern, a popular stop for all travelers in the region. The new city was named Raleigh, in honor of the first man to attempt to plant an English colony in the new country, Sir Walter Raleigh, who ironically never visited the area that was named for him.

The new state's constitution stressed the importance of education and universities; consequently, as soon as possible, the legislators set about the task of founding a university. With the goal of selecting a central location, they finally settled on New Hope Chapel. In November 1792, the name Chapel Hill was used in the trustees' report, and in February 1795 the university admitted its first student, Hinton James, of Wilmington.

In contrast, Durham is a much newer city. In the mid-1800s (the time of the founding of the city has never been established with certainty), Dr. Bartlett Snipes Durham granted a tract of four acres to the North Carolina Railroad for the purpose of establishing a depot in the area. The railroad named the new settlement for Dr. Durham. The city has since settled on the date of April 26, 1853, as the official birthday of the town because records indicate that a post office was established in the settlement on that date.

The region's soil was perfect for growing tobacco, and the tobacco industry began to thrive in the area. During the antebellum period, large plantations flourished here, and African slaves were transported to the area to help with farming tobacco and cotton crops.

North Carolina did not immediately side with the neighboring secessionist states in the period of deliberation leading up to the Civil War. In fact, the state stayed in the Union until the last possible moment before finally siding with the Confederacy. Once committed, however, North Carolina played an important part in the Civil War, and its regiments suffered the most casualties in the war.

Raleigh and Durham played important roles in the war. Because of the rich farming areas around Raleigh, when Gen. William T. Sherman made his famous march to the sea, he took a lot of food from the area for his troops. However, Raleigh was mercifully spared the burning that many of the cities suffered that were in Sherman's path.

Durham also was looted. But another very significant event occurred just outside Durham. In 1865, near the close of the war, seventeen days after Gen. Robert E. Lee made his surrender at Appomattox, Union general Sherman and Confederate general Joseph E. Johnston negotiated what came to be the largest surrender of the Civil War at a farm called Bennett Place. Today you can visit this important historical site and relive the events of that pivotal meeting.

While the generals were negotiating, the army troops were camped in and around Durham waiting the outcome of the negotiations. They enjoyed smoking the Brightleaf tobacco that was being grown in the area so much during these tense days that after they returned home, they ordered the tobacco by mail to enjoy on an ongoing basis. Thus, the tobacco industry began its heyday. Tobacco warehouses were built and prospered, and families like the Duke family began a period of economic prosperity that

The Globe Warehouse, circa 1886. (Courtesy Duke Homestead State Historic Site and Tobacco Museum)

has lasted to the present. Other industries sprang up near the tobacco mills, notably textile industries. Denim and other textiles became known and associated with the area.

Furthermore, after a period of no education in the years during and following the Civil War, North Carolina's educational institutions reopened, which renewed the state's long-standing commitment to education. The small Trinity College became Duke University in 1924 when it was moved to Durham from Randolf County, and in 1910, Dr. James E. Shepard founded North Carolina Central University, a liberal arts college for African-Americans.

In the late 1950s, Raleigh, Chapel Hill, and Durham were small Southern towns that came alive in the fall when students returned to the region's several campuses and when the state legislature was in session. In the late 1950s, events happened that ultimately changed the little towns into centers of scientific research and placed them on the cutting edge of technology worldwide.

Representatives from the three local universities (Duke University in Durham, North Carolina State University in Raleigh, and the University of North Carolina at Chapel Hill), along with local business and industry leaders, began to discuss the possibility of creating a park whose primary purpose would be to provide a center for research organizations. They wanted a place where economic development would attract companies from around the world that were dedicated to research and development in what were then new scientific areas.

In 1959 the park was created under the umbrella of the Research Triangle Foundation, and the ground-breaking ceremony welcomed the park's first tenet, the Research Triangle Institute. The concept of the triangle grew from the triangle formed geographically by the three universities. Thus, the region's nickname, the Triangle, was born. The institute remains the heart of the park and has become one of the world's premier research institutes. Each year the institute's 1,500 employees generate more than $100 million in research.

The 7,000 acres that currently comprise the park are in the center of the triangle that is composed of the three cities, Raleigh, Durham, and Chapel Hill, and its place in the center is appropriate, given what the park has done for the region over the past four decades. The sleepy little Southern cities are no more. Instead, the region is known internationally as a center for research, education, employment, sales, and quality of life. Currently, more than one hundred research and development facilities employ approximately 37,000 Triangle residents, and the combined annual salaries in Research Triangle Park amount to more than $1.2 billion.

This all adds up to a very high quality of life for Triangle residents. For example, the average household income is greater than $50,000. Economic growth has also allowed the region to develop a strong infrastructure, a rich cultural life, and a high per capita standard of living and education. The three universities alone have a combined enrollment of more than 60,000 students, and the Research Triangle is home to more Ph.D.'s per capita than any other place in the nation. It has become a strong, sophisticated, multicultural area, with people arriving daily from all over the world ready to make the region home.

The small, isolated Southern towns of Raleigh, Durham, and Chapel Hill are gone forever. In their place are three distinctive, prosperous cities connected to each other through the Research Triangle Park and hence, connected to the nation and to the world. Enhancing the cities is the new identity of an exciting area known as the Triangle. In spite of this growth and prosperity, the three cities have managed to retain the best of what is known as Southern warmth and hospitality—Southern charm.

Walk 1
City Scenes

General location: Explore Fayetteville Street Mall in the heart of downtown Raleigh as well as other downtown sights.

Special attractions: Fayetteville Street Mall, Moore Square Park, downtown Raleigh, a museum, an art gallery, and City Market with its gift stores, restaurants, and other shops.

Difficulty rating: Easy, flat, paved. Cobblestone sidewalk in the City Market portion of the walk only; the rest of the walk is sidewalk. All intersections have curb cuts and are equipped for the visually impaired, as well as for those in wheelchairs.

Distance: 1.3 miles.

Estimated time: 45 minutes.

City Scenes

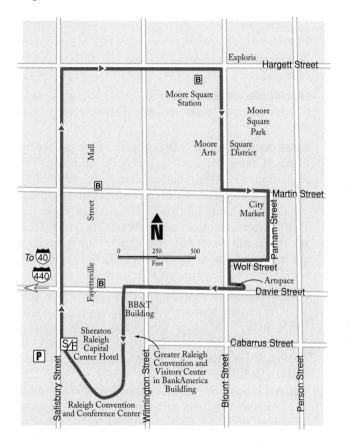

Services: Restaurants and wheelchair-accessible restrooms in the Sheraton Raleigh Capital Center Hotel, Artspace, Exploris, and Greater Raleigh Convention and Visitors Bureau.

Restrictions: Dogs must be leashed and their droppings picked up.

For more information: Contact the Greater Raleigh Convention and Visitors Bureau, Artspace, Exploris, or City Market.

Getting started: This walk begins at the Sheraton Raleigh Capital Center Hotel, 421 Salisbury Street. To reach the hotel from I–40/440, take exit 298B and go north on Saunders Street. Follow the signs to downtown Raleigh, veering right onto McDowell Street. Turn right onto Davie Street; in 1 block, turn right onto Salisbury Street, where you will find a parking garage on the right side of the street across from the Sheraton Raleigh Capital Center Hotel, as well as metered street parking.

Public transportation: Most buses in the Capital Area Transit (CAT) system go downtown: buses 1, 6, 11, 12, and 16. All of these run Monday through Saturday and travel either down Salisbury Street or to within a few blocks of the Raleigh Plaza Hotel. The Raleigh Trolley has a shuttle that circles Salisbury to Davie, Wilmington, Martin, Person, and Hargett Streets, around the capitol to the legislative building and back up Salisbury Street. The trolley runs every ten minutes during limited hours on weekdays, and there is a fare. Contact CAT for information about times, fares, and accessibility.

Overview: Raleigh is a beautiful old Southern city possessing a friendly, relaxed style people from the South, as well as others, have come to value. Simultaneously, the city is

The Birth of a Town

On one point the lawmakers were certain: The state's new capital was to be within 10 miles of Isaac Hunter's Tavern. Perhaps the refreshments there were a factor in their decision. They also wanted the capital near the center of the state and at the crossroads of major north–south and east–west highways.

The decision was not an easy one. Fayetteville, New Bern, Halifax, and Hillsborough all vied for the honor but eventually lost to the site in Wake County.

William Christmas surveyed the property. Working with commissioners appointed by the general assembly, he completed a plan for a city of 400 acres in just five days, including five public squares and 256, 1-acre building lots, which quickly sold.

In deference to the towns that lost to the Wake County site, the commissioners named the streets surrounding Union Square—the central square where the capitol is located—for the competing towns. Fayetteville is south of the capitol, and the first street south of Union Square is Fayetteville Street. Halifax Street points north toward the town bearing its name; New Bern and New Bern Street are east; and Hillsborough Street is west of Union Square going toward Hillsborough.

The lots were in an oak forest at the time of the city's founding; hence, Raleigh became the City of Oaks. Be sure to see the giant oak sculpture in Moore Square Park, a commemoration of Raleigh's nickname. You will pass by it on this walk through downtown Raleigh. On First Night Raleigh, celebrated every New Year's Eve, the acorn descends as the seconds are counted down to the new year.

Incidentally, a portion of what was thought to be Isaac Hunter's Tavern survived until the late 1970s just north of the capitol on Old Wake Forest Road.

comfortable with its growing reputation as a sophisticated, large multicultural city. You will not be disappointed in downtown Raleigh because a variety of experiences await you there, including a wealth of history alongside an expanding nightlife scene, trend-setting museums located next to oak tree–lined parks, and old brick-paved streets in the shadows of fifteen-plus–story skyscrapers.

Now it's time to walk. Most days, you will find a variety of food vendors on Fayetteville Street Mall, so grab the camera, walk out of the Sheraton Raleigh Capital Center Hotel, purchase some ice cream or an icy beverage from one of the vendors, and start walking.

The Walk

►Exit from the Sheraton Raleigh Capital Center Hotel on the Fayetteville Street Mall side of the hotel and turn left onto Fayetteville Street Mall, a pedestrian mall.

The Wake County Office Building is at 336 Fayetteville Street Mall, and an electronic branch of Wake County Public Library is at number 334. Benches, lily-filled pools, and fountains line the mall, and you will see people playing checkers on inlaid checkerboard tops of picnic tables.

Number 316 is the Wake County Courthouse. Wheelchair access is at the Salisbury Street entrance. The 1874 Century Post Office at number 314 was the first federal project in North Carolina following the Civil War. The red brick, 1874 Briggs Building at number 220 was originally Briggs Hardware. It is Raleigh's first skyscraper and the only late nineteenth-century unaltered commercial building. To reach the fourth floor, the top floor of this early skyscraper, requires ninety-one steps. The building is

Walkers and shoppers at City Market. (Courtesy Peter Damroth/ Greater Raleigh Convention and Visitors Bureau)

home to various organizations, including Special Olympics and the Raleigh History Museum. Notice the red brick facade and the decorative lion heads.

The North Carolina State Bar Association at number 208 has a distinctive arched entranceway.

➤Turn right onto Hargett Street. The Moore Square Arts District begins on this street. Notice the large brick tower. It is part of the 1988 Moore Square Station, home to the public transit terminal and a parking garage. Most area buses can be accessed through Moore Square.

Number 128, the 1912 Montague Building is a Raliegh Historic Property. Home to several offices and restaurants, it was the first commercial building in the Moore Square Park area.

At 112 Blount Street near the intersection of Blount and Hargett Streets is a massive structure called Exploris. Opened only recently, Exploris is a state-of-the-art children's museum designed to encourage young people to make connections with people of the world.

➤Turn right onto Blount Street. Moore Square Park is on the left. Cross the street and enter the park to get a close-up view of the copper acorn. At midnight on New Year's Eve, crowds gather in the park to watch the acorn being lowered to start the new year. It is Raleigh's reminder of the city's nickname, City of Oaks.

This park is one of the four public squares laid out in the original plans for the city; only two of the four squares remain as parks. As you walk through the park, notice the wall murals under the massive oaks. Return to Blount Street to continue your walk.

➤At the intersection of Blount and Martin Streets, cross and turn left, following Martin Street.

City Market and Moore Square

The Spanish-mission style City Market, built in 1914, was once a place for local farmers to showcase their fresh fruits and vegetables as well as small livestock such as chickens and rabbits. Notice the 9-foot-wide cobblestone sidewalks and the wide overhangs on the roofs of the buildings. These wide sidewalks and expansive eaves provided room and shelter for farmers to display their products. Inside, yesteryear's shoppers could buy fresh fish from the fishmongers or quality cuts of beef and pork at the market's butcher shops.

Farmers and members of their families came into town to City Market and spent the day. They spread picnic lunches on the lawn in Moore Square Park, and women laid out clothing on the grass and held rummage sales. The farmers' livestock, including horses and mules were watered at a large fountain on the square. All in all, it was an important day for everyone—vendors and shoppers.

When the mid-1900s brought grocery stores, along with superhighways to access the suburbs, the need for City Market declined. It was sold and then not used for some time. In the 1980s, town officials became interested in downtown renewal and invested in renovation of the market. This made it possible for shops and restaurants to locate there.

Today City Market is a bustling center of trendy restaurants, art studios, boutiques, offices, and even a microbrewery, Greenshield's Brewery and Pub. During the day, state government workers and other downtown Raleigh businesspeople meet at the restaurants for lunch. Tourists flock to the ice cream stores, coffee bars, and gift shops or simply browse while walking along the beautiful cobblestone streets.

➤Turn right onto Parham Street. You are now on the cobblestone streets and sidewalks of City Market.

➤Turn right onto Wolf Street. Walk to the end of this short cobblestone street.

➤Turn left onto Blount Street. At 201 Davie Street, Artspace's bright yellow banners announce the arts center's entrance at the intersection of Blount and Davie Streets. Turn left at this intersection to enter Artspace, a visual arts center with bright purple and blue walls; open, functional stairwells; and artists' studios.

Artspace's mission is to enrich the community by bringing artists, the creative process, the artwork, and the public together. The Upfront Gallery displays artists' works. Up to forty-six artists can use studio space in Artspace. You can observe artists at work in their studios, but individual artist studio hours vary. Arts programs, including lectures, demonstrations, gallery talks, and arts classes are available. Contact the office for information.

➤From the Davie entrance to Artspace, turn right onto Davie Street. The Raleigh skyline is visible to the right and left on this portion of the walk. The sidewalk here has some rough spots. Watch carefully, especially if you are in a wheelchair or pushing a stroller.

➤At the pedestrian crossing for Fayetteville Street Mall, turn left back onto the mall.

➤Continue walking toward the Raleigh Convention and Conference Center, the large structure at the end of the mall.

Two skyscrapers dominate this end of the mall on the left, One Hanover Square, which houses BankAmerica, and Two Hanover Square, which is home to Bankers Branch and Trust (BB&T). The BankAmerica building is

Artists at work in Artspace, City Market, Raleigh. (Courtesy Peter Damroth/Greater Raleigh Convention and Visitors Bureau)

home to the Greater Raleigh Convention and Visitors Bureau. Enter this building and go to the fifteenth floor to enter the bureau. Here you will find a knowledgeable, friendly staff offering free brochures, schedules, and other helpful information for your stay in Raleigh.

The Raleigh Convention and Conference Center is at the end of this portion of Fayetteville Street Mall. It anchors one end of the mall and the state capitol anchors the other end of the mall.

▶In front of the Convention and Conference Center, turn and walk back along the mall. The Sheraton Raleigh Capital Center Hotel, where you began your walk, is on the left.

Raleigh's Namesake

North Carolina's capital is named for Sir Walter Raleigh, who it appears was never in the state. Nevertheless, in 1792 members of the general assembly named the capital for him because he was so instrumental in establishing colonies in the New World, the most famous of which is the Lost Colony.

In April 1587, Raleigh sent colonists to Roanoke Island led by Gov. John White. By August supplies were low and White returned to England to restock. Before he left the colonists agreed to carve a cross on a tree if there was trouble. When White returned, the only signs of the colony were the letters C-R-O carved on a tree; the name CROATOAN; and the sign of a cross carved near where the houses had been. The colonists' fate is still unknown.

Raleigh was a character as colorful as the spellings of his name, which he spelled Rawleyghe, Rauley, and Ralegh. However, he never used Raleigh, the spelling of the city that is his namesake. He was a war hero, explorer, adventurer, and court favorite of Queen Elizabeth. The story of Raleigh using his coat to cover a puddle of water for the queen has never been proven, but fits well with the dashing Sir Walter.

Regretfully, his relationship with the queen ended sadly. When she learned he had secretly married one of her ladies-in-waiting, Elizabeth Throckmorton, she had them locked in the Tower of London. Although later released, Raleigh remained exiled from her court.

The situation worsened for Raleigh when Elizabeth was succeeded by James I, who believed Raleigh was plotting with Spain. After more imprisonments in the tower, releases, and scheduled hangings, Raleigh finally was beheaded on October 29, 1618, on orders of James I.

The city that bears his name is a proud symbol of his love for adventure and his charming personality.

Walk 2
Capitol Walk

General location: Explore Raleigh and North Carolina's history in a walk that takes you around the grounds of and into North Carolina's state capitol building.

Special attractions: Historic landmarks, state capitol building, Union Square.

Difficulty rating: Easy, flat, and on sidewalks.

Distance: 1.5 miles.

Estimated time: 45 minutes.

Services: Restaurants along Salisbury and other streets bordering the capitol and along Fayetteville Street Mall; accessible restrooms on the second floor of the capitol via the elevator. Water fountain on Union Square between the east and south lawns.

Capitol Walk

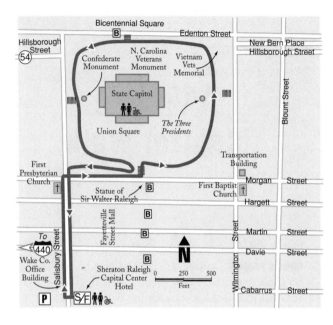

Restrictions: Dogs must be leashed and their droppings picked up. The capitol is closed on Thanksgiving, Christmas, and New Year's Day.

For more information: Contact the Capital Area Visitor Center, the North Carolina State Capitol, or the Greater Raleigh Convention and Visitors Bureau.

Getting started: This walk begins at the Sheraton Raleigh Captial Center Hotel at 421 Salisbury Street. To reach the hotel from I–40/440, take exit 298B and go north on Saunders Street. Follow the signs to downtown Raleigh, veering right onto McDowell Street. Turn right onto Davie Street, go 1 block, and turn right onto Salisbury Street, where you will find a parking garage across from the Sheraton Raleigh Capital Center Hotel and metered street parking.

Public transportation: Most buses in the Capital Area Transit (CAT) system go downtown: buses 1, 6, 11, 12, and 16. These run Monday through Saturday and travel either down Salisbury Street or to within a few blocks of the Sheraton Raleigh Capital Center Hotel. The Raleigh Trolley has a shuttle that circles Salisbury to Davie, Wilmington, Martin, Person, and Hargett Streets, around the capitol to the legislative building, and back up Salisbury Street. The trolley runs every ten minutes during limited hours on weekdays; there is a fare. Contact CAT for information about times, fares, and accessibility.

Overview: The North Carolina state capitol is the heart of this walk and the heart of Raleigh.

Twice in its history the capital of the state almost failed to be located in Raleigh.

When the governing bodies of the new state of North Carolina were trying to decide where to locate the seat of government in the late 1700s, New Bern, Fayetteville, Hillsborough, and other cities vied for the honor. Raleigh was chosen, and a state house was completed in 1794. The new state house served as the center of state government, a community center, and a place for religious services until it burned on June 21, 1831. The state house was completely destroyed in the fire except for a few state papers, and the location of the state capital was debated again.

Since Raleigh had no industry, no waterway, and no railroad, planners felt another location would be preferable; however, Raleigh was again the choice, possibly because of the site's history as the chosen location, and the capitol you see on this walk was completed in 1840.

Your walk will take you around the capitol grounds called Union Square. Here you will relive moments in North Carolina's history and see statues of some of the state's notable leaders. In addition, the many statues and memorials on Union Square depict the uniforms of the soldiers from the various wars and the equipment they carried, illustrating the evolution of the technology of warfare.

Inside the capitol you will see the rooms where state government was conducted until 1963. The state's legislative building is located a few blocks from the capitol.

The Walk

►Walk out of the Sheraton Raleigh Capital Center Hotel on the Salisbury Street side of the hotel and turn right onto Salisbury Street. You will pass number 337, the Waverly F. Akins Wake County Office Building. The Wake County Courthouse is on the right just beyond the county office building. A curved sidewalk in front of the pink granite First Union Building lets wheelchair users and those pushing strollers avoid the curb dropoffs there.

Number 112, the First Presbyterian Church, was built in 1900. It is a Raleigh Historic Property and is registered by the Presbyterian Historical Society. The church's angled entry faces Union Square, site of the state capitol. The church is an irregularly shaped Romanesque revival–style red brick building with an open bell tower. Look up at the bell tower and at its copper roof. After the 1831 State House fire, the state supreme court met in the church from 1831 to 1840, when the new capitol was completed.

Statue of Sir Walter Raleigh on Fayetteville Street Mall. (Courtesy Peter Damroth/Greater Raleigh Convention and Visitors Bureau)

➤Turn right onto Morgan Street. You are now in front of the capitol, which sits on Union Square.

➤In the center of the block look to your right down Fayetteville Street Mall at the statue of Raleigh's namesake, Sir Walter Raleigh.

➤Cross Morgan Street, using the pedestrian crosswalk in the middle of the block. You are now in front of the capitol and at the southern entrance to Union Square, the grounds that the capitol sits on and home to a collection of statues and monuments.

The first statue you see to the left down Morgan Street is the *Women of the Confederacy.* Donated by Confederate veteran Col. Ashley Horne, this seated woman reads to her young son, who carries a musket. The work commemorates and honors the hardships women faced during the war.

➤Take either the steps or the ramp straight ahead that lead onto the grounds of Union Square. Many large oak trees shade the grounds.

Note: For those in wheelchairs or pushing strollers, this is the only accessible entrance to Union Square and the capitol.

To the left is a statue of Charles Brantley Aycock, governor of the state from 1901 to 1905. Aycock is known for his emphasis on education, so it is fitting that the monument was sponsored by schoolchildren, friends, and educators.

In the center of this entrance to the capitol is a bronze statue of George Washington, flanked by two cannons that were cast in France before the American Revolution. The statue is a gift from the town of Edenton, about 100 miles east of Raleigh. The statue of Washington was intended to replace a sculpture of Washington destroyed when the State House burned in 1831. The first statue on the square, it was unveiled on July 4, 1857. Steps lead to the cannons and to the statue.

To the right of the Washington statue is a statue of Zebulon B. Vance, governor of the state during the tumultuous years of the Civil War. He was elected governor in 1862, reelected in 1864, but was removed from office and imprisoned when Union officials took over at the end of the war. After his prison term, he resumed his law practice and was eventually elected to a third term as governor in 1876. Before completing this term, he was elected in 1879 to the U.S. Senate, where he served until his death in 1894.

►Continue walking around the grounds of Union Square, in a counterclockwise direction, following the street signs.

Of Interest

The Presidents North Carolina Gave the Nation

On the east side of the capitol is one of the most famous statues on the grounds, the bronze statue known as *The Three Presidents.* It depicts three North Carolina natives: James Knox Polk, eleventh president, from 1845 to 1849; Andrew Jackson, seventh president, from 1829 to 1837; and Andrew Johnson, seventeenth president, from 1865 to 1869. James K. Polk, to the left, is seated and holds a map to commemorate his expansion of our national boundaries. To the right is Andrew Johnson; he holds the U.S. Constitution, which he defended. Johnson was born just south of this statue behind the present justice building. His birthplace is located in Mordecai Historic Park, which you can see on Walk 4. Andrew Jackson on horseback dominates the trio.

You should now be parallel to Wilmington Street and be able to see the First Baptist Church across Wilmington.

You are now on the east side of the capitol; across Wilmington is the Transportation Building. *The Three Presidents,* a bronze statue in the center of the east entrance grounds, commemorates the presidents North Carolina gave the nation.

➤Two large fountains behind *The Three Presidents* flank the main capitol entrance, which you can enter now.

Of Interest

The North Carolina State Capitol

The capitol standing on Union Square is not the original building. The original structure was a two-story brick building called the State House. Completed in 1796, just twenty years after the signing of the Declaration of Independence, it served as the seat of state government until it burned in 1831. Ironically, the fire occurred during the installation of a zinc roof, which was intended to make the building fireproof.

The fire destroyed the building and most of its contents. A much-loved marble statue of George Washington sculpted by Antonio Canova in the early 1800s was also destroyed. The building's heavy dome, which had been added during improvements to the State House to showcase the sculpture, collapsed and crushed it.

The general assembly quickly authorized the building of a new, larger capitol designed like the old State House with its cross shape and central, domed rotunda. The neoclassic design includes many Grecian architectural details. The exterior Doric columns are modeled after those of the Parthenon, and the honeysuckle crown on top of the dome exhibits features of ancient Greek temples.

The exterior walls of the capitol are built of gneiss, a form of granite quarried in southeastern Raleigh. Interior walls are stone and brick, and the gallery overhanging the second floor of the rotunda is masonry, making them virtually fireproof. Most interior and exterior features of the capitol are original.

In the early 1900s, the Italians gave North Carolina a plaster cast of Canova's working model for the sculpture of Washington. Seventy years later, Italian artist Romano Vio used the model to create the marble sculpture that is now the central feature of the rotunda.

Note: A wheelchair entrance to the capitol is located on the south side of the building.

Stand in the center of the rotunda and look up for a good view of the gallery and the interior of the dome. The statue of George Washington stands in the center of the rotunda. Busts of North Carolinians adorn the rotunda, along with plaques honoring North Carolina people and events.

The governor's office is located on this floor and is occasionally open for viewing. Other offices on this floor not open for touring are the former offices of state treasurer, the secretary of state, and the supreme court chambers. These offices are now used by the governor's staff.

➤Walk behind the statue of Washington to ascend the stairs; elevators are also available. If you do take the stairs, notice the chips in the steps. According to legend, these chips were caused by post—Civil War carpetbaggers rolling barrels of whiskey down the steps.

At the top of the stairs, the state senate room, which was used from 1840 to 1961, is on the left. Be sure to notice the

Ionic columns, the large fireplaces at the rear of the room, the wooden desks, the ornate frame with the lithograph of the Marquis de Lafayette viewing the statue of George Washington, and the red carpet with bright gold stars. The walls of this room are painted Carolina blue.

Across the rotunda is the house of representatives chamber, modeled after a Greek amphitheater with Corinthian-style columns. Note the podiums and desks; the Thomas Sully portrait of Washington, which was one of the few items saved from the 1831 fire; and the red carpet with the thirty-one-star pattern symbolizing the thirty-one states in the nation at the time the carpet was designed. Many details in the chamber, such as the window shades, are reproductions made to resemble the originals.

The third floor of the capitol contains the original state library, in use from 1840 to 1888. Many of the room's details, such as the colors, and some of the furniture, have been re-created based on its 1856 appearance as detailed in state archives records.

➤Exit the capitol via the door you entered, and turn left. The Vietnam Veterans' Memorial to your right near the intersection of Wilmington and Edenton Streets was dedicated May 1987. The monument depicts two soldiers carrying a wounded comrade for medical assistance.

➤Follow the sidewalk to the north side of the capitol; Edenton Street is on your right.

The North Carolina Veterans' Monument is the focal point of the north side of the capitol. Dedicated in May 1990, this monument honors veterans of both world wars and the Korean War. It was the first marker on the grounds to honor these veterans. A bronze eternal flame and a bronze Lady Liberty, holding a palm representing victory and peace, tops the monument. Flags of each branch of service accent the monument.

North Carolina's state capitol as seen from Bicentennial Square. (Courtesy Peter Damroth/Greater Raleigh Convention and Visitors Bureau)

Across Edenton Street, Bicentennial Square is home to the museum of natural sciences, the museum of history, and the legislative building, which you can visit on Walk 3 in this book.

►Follow the sidewalk to the west side of the capitol paralleling Salisbury Street. The first statue you will see on the west lawn is of Henry Lawson Wyatt, from Edgecombe County, east of Raleigh. Killed near Hampton Roads, Virginia, on June 10, 1861, he was the first Confederate soldier to die in battle in the Civil War.

Across the lawn is a statue of Ens. Worth Bagley, born in Raleigh in 1874, who was the first American officer killed in the Spanish-American War. The Spanish naval deck gun was captured in 1898 and mounted here in 1908.

The tall monument at the Salisbury Street entrance to Union Square is the Confederate Monument. Flanked by two cannons, the monument commemorates the large number of North Carolina soldiers who were killed in the Civil War. Almost one-quarter of Confederate casualties were North Carolinians. This statue also commemorates North Carolina soldiers' tenacity during the war with the inscription FIRST AT BETHEL—LAST AT APPOMATTOX, recalling the first and last battles of that war.

►Follow the sidewalk around Union Square. Return to the south lawn and exit Union Square.

►Turn right onto Morgan and walk one-half block to Salisbury Street.

►Turn left onto Salisbury to return to the Sheraton Raleigh Capital Center Hotel.

Walk 3
Government and Museums

General location: The North Carolina State Legislative Building and two of North Carolina's most famous museums are the focal points of this walk.

Special attractions: North Carolina Museum of Science, North Carolina Museum of Natural History, the state legislative building, Capital Area Visitor Center, the North Carolina executive mansion.

Difficulty rating: Easy, flat, sidewalks.

Distance: 1.3 miles.

Estimated time: 45 minutes.

Services: Accessible restrooms in the museums, the visitor center, and in the legislative building when they are open.

Government and Museums

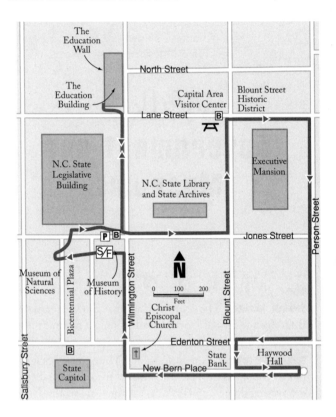

A small cafeteria is in the basement of the labor building adjacent to the museum of natural sciences. The museum has a cafe, and refreshments are available in the basement of the legislative building. Gift shops are in the museums. A picnic area is located on Lane Street between Wilmington and Blount Streets and across from the Capital Area Visitor Center.

Restrictions: Dogs must be leashed and droppings picked up. The museum of history is closed on Mondays; the museum of natural sciences is closed on state holidays.

For more information: Contact the Capital Area Visitor Center, the Greater Raleigh Convention and Visitors Bureau, the museum of natural science, the museum of history.

Getting started: This walk begins at the North Carolina Museum of History at 4 Edenton Street. To reach the museum from I-440, take exit 3 and go east on Hillsborough Street. At McDowell Street, turn left; turn right onto Jones Street. An underground parking lot is on the right below the museum of history at Wilmington and Jones Streets.

Public transportation: Capital Area Transportation (CAT) buses 1, 2, 4, 6, 8, 12, and 20 go to the museum of history. The Raleigh Trolley runs a shuttle every ten minutes on weekdays. Contact CAT for information about times, fares, and accessibility.

Overview: You can spend an hour or a day in either of the museums on this walk. The museum of history offers a wealth of information about the history of North Carolina and its people. For example, if North Carolina sports interest you, be sure to visit the North Carolina Sports Hall of Fame in the museum. North Carolina folklife is showcased

in an ongoing exhibit titled "The Spirit of Community."
Also, "The Past in Progress: Gathering the Treasures of
North Carolina" depicts significant events in the state's
history.

The museum of natural sciences showcases the state's
natural resources. In this building, you can visit a mine,
walk through a wetland and a marsh, view the variety of
snakes that inhabit the state, and visit a discovery room to
explore North Carolina's natural life.

Walk inside the state legislative building to observe the
legislature in action. You will be in the center of the state's
governing bodies when you visit this building. Later in the
walk you will see the exterior of the Victorian mansion
that North Carolina's governor calls home.

North Carolina life, its people, its history, and its government are showcased in this walk. The staff at the
Greater Raleigh Convention and Visitors Bureau coined a
phrase, "You can see the whole state from here" (meaning
Raleigh). They could just as accurately say, "You can see
the whole state on this walk."

The Walk

Note: An elevator takes you from the underground parking
area below the museum of history to the main floor or you
can enter the museum from Bicentennial Plaza. Wheelchair access to the museum from Bicentennial Plaza is off
Jones Street at Fletcher Garden Plaza. At the replica of
the Liberty Bell at Fletcher Garden Plaza off Jones Street,
enter the museum through the glass doors and take the elevator to the main floor of the museum.

➤After visiting the museum of history, walk out onto Bicentennial Plaza.

The State Legislative Building

Until 1963 the North Carolina General Assembly met in the state capitol. In 1963 the assembly moved to the new state legislative building, which houses the legislative branch of government.

Edward Durell Stone, architect for the John F. Kennedy Center for the Performing Arts in Washington, D.C., designed the building. Walkers who have visited the Kennedy Center will see resemblances between the structures. The building is a marble-faced structure, encompassed by a colonnade of square columns, which give it a classical look. The pyramidal glass domes that serve as roofs and the third-floor roof gardens planted with flowering shrubs add a distinctively modern look to this regal structure.

The building contains the North Carolina senate and house chambers, meeting spaces for committees, offices for senators and representatives and their clerical support, a post office, a chapel, a library, space for media and press conferences, room for public meetings, and public balconies for observation of the senate and house chambers.

Inside the main doors, the red-carpeted staircase leading to the third-floor viewing areas for the senate and house chambers dominates the view. Visitors can ascend the stairs to view the legislative chambers, enter the auditorium, or enter the roof area.

The building's interior is a maze divided into four identical quadrants with four identical courtyards. Visitors, as well as seasoned employees, frequently get lost in the interior of the building, which is why it is suggested you return to the main entrance and walk around the exterior of the building. Jokes about lost people in the building have become legend, including the story about the legislative aide who advises visitors to bring a bag of popcorn and to leave a trail.

The ornate architecture of North Carolina's Executive Mansion. (Courtesy Peter Damroth/Greater Raleigh Convention and Visitors Bureau)

➤Cross the plaza, and you will be in front of the museum of natural sciences. North Carolina's oldest museum, it is on the National Register of Historic Places. The new museum, which contains eight new exhibits on marine life, North Carolina habitats, insects, fossils, and much more, is next door.

➤Return to Bicentennial Plaza after your visit to the museum of natural sciences and turn left toward Jones Street. The building directly ahead of you and across the street is the North Carolina State Legislative Building. You can enter through the main doors. Be sure to notice the 28-foot terrazzo mosaic of the state seal bearing the state motto, "To Be Rather Than to Seem."

➤After your visit, return to the Jones Street entrance.

➤Turn left onto Jones Street and walk to its intersection with Wilmington Street.

➤Turn left onto Wilmington Street and walk 1 block to its intersection with Lane Street.

➤Cross Lane Street. The Education Building is on your left. The Education Wall is on the side of the building opposite Wilmington Street.

➤Follow the sidewalk around in front of the Education Building to reach the intersection of Lane and Wilmington Streets.

➤Retrace your steps along Wilmington Street. You are walking parallel to the legislative building, which is across the street on your right.

➤At the intersection of Jones and Wilmington Streets, turn left, following Jones Street.

The North Carolina State Archives and the North Carolina State Library are on your left. The state library

Of Interest

The Education Wall

The Education Wall of the Education Building celebrates the people of North Carolina with wall art featuring quotations by North Carolinians.

Artist Vernon Pratt and writer Georgann Eubanks turned this wall into an educational experience. Benches in front of the wall provide information about the authors of the wall's quotations.

Wisdom from North Carolina women, Cherokees, musicians, the sight-impaired, politicians, slaves, and others on subjects including art, literature, music, education, and history are collected here.

If you are walking with young children, bring paper and crayons so they can take rubbings of the benches and wall elements.

was established in 1812, and the Division of Archives and History was organized in 1903. Those in wheelchairs who wish to visit the library or archives building should use the Blount Street entrance ramp. To reach this entrance, follow Jones Street to the next intersection, which is Blount Street, turn left, and look for the ramp.

The state archives contains documents from state agencies, county records from the colonial period to 1910, and military collections, among others, all of which are accessible via a research room.

The state library serves the state government and general assembly; provides braille materials and audiotape books and large-print books for the blind; holds extensive genealogical and local history materials; directs a statewide summer reading program; and coordinates the annual Quiz Bowl.

➤After your visit, exit onto Jones Street and turn left.

➤Turn left onto Blount Street. The North Carolina executive mansion is across the street, and the Capital Area Visitor Center is at number 301.

The visitor center has wheelchair-accessible restrooms; information and brochures about the capital and surrounding area; a short slide show about the sites in Raleigh; plus maps, directions, and other information. The center is located in the historic Andrews-London House. It was built in 1918 for banker Graham Harris Andrews, who became Raleigh's mayor in 1939.

➤At the intersection of Blount and Lane Streets, turn right following Lane Street toward the executive mansion on your right. The Blount Street Historic District begins here, and several houses along this portion of Lane are historic.

As you walk along the brick sidewalk in front of the mansion along Lane Street, you can look through the wrought-iron gate at the gardens, porches, and architecture of the mansion.

➤Turn right onto Person Street. The brick sidewalk ends at the end of the next block, and a concrete sidewalk resumes.

Note: For those in wheelchairs or pushing strollers, use care as you approach the 1-inch step-up at the intersection of Jones and Person Streets. You can wheel around it, but watch for oncoming traffic before you do so.

➤Turn right onto Edenton Street.

➤Turn left onto Blount Street.

The North Carolina Executive Mansion

This Victorian mansion, completed in 1891 after nine years of construction, was designed as a governor's residence. Before the mansion was built, governors lived in rented property and hotels. Gov. Thomas J. Jarvis (1879–85) saw the need for a place to entertain, and led the state to build the mansion.

This Queen Anne–style, thirty-room mansion has accommodated twenty-five governors and was once described by Pres. Franklin D. Roosevelt as the most beautiful executive mansion interior in the country.

Finding it somewhat ornate for modern tastes, some North Carolinians wanted to replace the mansion with a contemporary one. However, the historical value of the mansion prevailed, and it was retained and restored.

As you walk around the exterior of the mansion, note that some bricks used in the mansion and the walkways bear the signatures of the prisoners who made them.

An interesting legend persists about Daniel G. Fowle, the first governor to occupy the mansion. Governor Fowle used his own furnishings because construction costs were over budget. A widower, he ordered an oversized but short mahogany bed, which tradition says he slept in with his young son. Governors used this bed until 1969, when Gov. Robert W. Scott found it too short for his comfort. He replaced it with a new bed and put Governor Fowle's bed in storage on the third floor.

One night at about ten o'clock, the Scotts heard several knocking sounds in the wall where the old bed had stood and concluded that it was the ghost of Governor Fowle wanting his bed back. Today the bed, along with other artifacts, is stored in the Division of Archives and History.

Tours of the home are limited. Contact the Capital Area Visitor Center for information.

➤Turn left onto New Bern Place. This small, shaded cul-de-sac contains residential houses, many of which are historical.

Haywood Hall on the left at number 211, now a museum, is the oldest residence built within the original city limits that is still on its original site. This home has changed very little since its construction in 1799; tours are available.

Built by then state treasurer John Haywood, Haywood Hall was the site of political meetings, balls, other significant social events, and large breakfasts for the general assembly. Later in this walk you will see Christ Episcopal Church, where Haywood and his family worshiped. You can imagine how this house, located so close to the capital and the church, shaped life for the Haywoods in the early 1900s.

➤Return along the other side of New Bern Place and continue along New Bern Place. Number 123 is the original North Carolina State Bank, now the State Employees Credit Union. Chartered in 1810, it was created as a depository for all state money when it seemed the British navy would attack the North Carolina coast during the war of 1812. Before this, there was no state banking institution. The bank's first president, Col. William Polk, made his home in the building.

Observe the handmade brick and stuccoed brick columns. The interior retains many original fixtures, including mantels, doors, and a circular stairway. At the foot of the stairs is a display of some of the items found in and around the building: nails, horse bits, a penny whistle, and a letter opener among others. Also, look at the ornate lighting fixtures.

➤Continue walking up New Bern Place. A wrought-iron fence surrounds the courtyard of Christ Episcopal Church at 120 Edenton Street. Established in 1821 and on the Raleigh list of historic sites and a National Historic Landmark, the church was built in the Gothic revival style using locally quarried stone.

Be sure to notice the gilded weather cock on the top of the church's bell tower. Set in place by a little boy, it has an amusing legend. It is said that as Gen. William Tecumseh Sherman approached Raleigh during the Civil War, the last of the Confederate troops retreated from the city. Desperate for food, they pillaged as they went. The weather cock at Christ Episcopal Church, so the story goes, was the only chicken left in Raleigh.

►Turn right onto Wilmington Street. Two blocks down is Jones Street and the parking garage where you began the walk.

Walk 4
Historic
Neighborhoods

General location: The Victorian neighborhoods of Oak-wood, Blount Street, and Mordecai Historic Park.

Special attractions: Grand historic homes, many listed on the National Register of Historic Places, and Mordecai Historic Park.

Difficulty rating: Easy, flat, paved sidewalks.

Distance: 1.5 miles.

Estimated time: 45 minutes.

Services: You will find restrooms and a gift shop in Morde-cai Historic Park, when it is open. Refreshments and rest-rooms are available at the Krispy Kreme Doughnut shop on Person Street. There is a picnic area on Polk Street between

Historic Neighborhoods

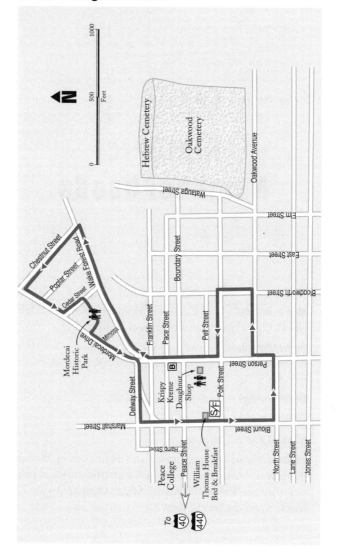

Blount and Person Streets. Few other services are available along this walk.

Restrictions: Dogs must be leashed and droppings picked up. Mordecai Historic Park is closed on Tuesdays and holidays; admission is charged.

For more information: Contact Mordecai Historic Park.

Getting started: From I–440, take exit 4A onto Wade Avenue. Go east, toward downtown Raleigh. You will drive through residential and shopping areas along Wade Street. Go 2.5 miles and turn left onto Peace Street. Turn right onto Blount Street. The William Thomas House Bed and Breakfast, where you begin the walk, is at number 530. A visitor parking lot is located at the intersection of Polk and Wilmington Streets. To reach the visitor parking lot, turn left onto Blount Street and then right onto Polk Street. Guests of the William Thomas House Bed and Breakfast can use its parking lot. If you are not a guest of the Thomas House, call first to make sure parking is available. On-street parking is available, but fills up fast on weekdays; you might try side street parking. Parking is easier to find on weekends.

Public transportation: Capital Area Transit bus 1 travels Blount Street and stops at the intersection of Person and Pace Streets.

Overview: History as well as grand homes await you on this walk through Oakwood and Mordecai Historic Park. In addition, you can take a short ¼-mile side trip through Oakwood Cemetery, rich in Civil War history as well as history related to the city of Raleigh. Taking a walk through historic Oakwood lets you see an urban community that has moved full circle from its founding in the 1870s, to its decline in the 1920s and 1930s, and then to its revitalization one hundred years later.

On the northern outskirts of the city, Oakwood Cemetery—established in 1869—became the namesake of the neighborhood, for both are named for the City of Oaks. Builders like Thomas H. Briggs, whose hardware store still stands on Fayetteville Street Mall, and Richard Stanhope Pullen, a developer, began to eye the land for residential development. At about the same time, heirs of the Moses Mordecai (pronounced MOR-de-kee) estate just to the north of the area began to sell some of their properties. In 1875, after Henry Lane's death, some of the property was subdivided and developed into a suburban residential community. City commissioners began to extend the boundaries of the city, which had remained unchanged since 1857. The Oakwood and Blount (pronounced blunt) Street neighborhoods boasted some of the larger and more expensive homes in the city. The area quickly became popular with bankers, railroad engineers, merchants, and cotton and tobacco brokers.

Oakwood remained a prosperous and popular area until after World War I, when cars enabled residents to move to more distant suburbs. The area began a decline; some houses were damaged and vandalized. Many that remained were considered too gaudy for modern tastes with their gables, turrets, cupolas, and high-pitched roofs. Some were converted to boardinghouses and apartments. Long-term plans for the area included leveling many of the homes to make way for an expressway.

However, in the late 1960s, young professionals were attracted to the neighborhood, and restoration began in earnest. The Society for the Preservation of Historic Oakwood was formed, and today attractive street signs are proudly displayed at the borders of this historic district.

Walk 4

The Mordecai family's influence was a factor in the development of Oakwood. The Mordecai home, which you can also visit on this walk, documents the influence of this prominent family. Mordecai Historic Park features a replica of a nineteenth-century village street and provides unique glimpses into life in Raleigh during that time. Mordecai house and the Oakwood community are on the National Register of Historic Places and the Raleigh Historic Properties Commission Register.

The Walk

Note: The Tarheel State Walkers, a local walking club, designed a walk through Raleigh neighborhoods; some of that information is used in this walk. The Society for the Preservation of Historic Oakwood collected information on the area's homes when it designed its walk, and some of that information appears as well.

➤From the driveway of the William Thomas House Bed and Breakfast, turn left onto Blount Street.

The William Thomas House is one of two historic bed-and-breakfasts in historic Oakwood. You will pass by the other one, the Oakwood Inn Bed and Breakfast on Bloodworth Street, later in this walk. The William Thomas House, formerly the Gray Fish Richardson House, was built about 1881 for Robert Gray, an attorney. It is a two-and-one-half-story Victorian home with porches on either side of the front gable.

The Queen Anne–style Lucy Catherine Capeheart House is on the corner of Polk and Blount Streets. The Office of Administrative Hearings for the state of North Carolina is located here.

Across the street, a roadside marker calls your attention to number 407, the Alexander B. Andrews House. Andrews, a railroad builder, financier, and vice president of Southern Railroad, bought this home of cross-gabled Italianate architecture from the Heck family in 1921 and lived there until he died in 1946. Colonel and Mrs. Heck built the house in 1870. Note the cupolas, the columns, and the large windows of this cream-colored house with rich brown trim.

➤Turn left onto North Street. Across the way at 300 Blount Street is the home of the lieutenant governor of North Carolina. The executive mansion is 1 block south.

➤At the end of North Street, turn left onto Person Street.

➤Turn right onto Oakwood Avenue, which is the beginning of historic Oakwood.

Number 304 is the Marcellus Parker House. Parker, a cotton and tobacco broker, lived in this, the earliest home on Oakwood Avenue. Notice the large shuttered doors, a feature of the Second Empire style. Also, notice the wraparound porch and bay window at number 312, the J. T. Moore House.

Across the street at number 315 is the Williams-Stamps House and at number 317 is the Williams Primrose House, built by the first female bank president in North Carolina, Merriam Williams, president of the State National Bank. For a time she and her daughters lived in these houses, which later became rental properties.

Number 318, the M. V. Bingham House, is a lovely, classic Victorian cottage. Note the arched windows on the front porch.

➤Turn left onto Bloodworth Street.

Oakwood Cemetery

You may continue on Oakwood Avenue at its intersection with Bloodworth Street to visit Oakwood Cemetery at number 701. The entrance to the cemetery is 3 blocks away. Raleigh's oldest, private nonprofit cemetery was established in 1869 and contains the graves of influential citizens of Raleigh and greater North Carolina, including governors and other officials. The Mordecai family donated the land in 1866, and a section of the cemetery is reserved for them.

The cemetery is on a hillside covered with oaks, cedars, azaleas, wide lawns, and paved streets, making it attractive and easy to wander through.

An intriguing part of the cemetery is the Confederate Cemetery. More than 2,800 Confederate dead were moved here when the Unionists ordered their bodies removed from graves near Pettigrew Hospital to make room for a national cemetery.

One year later the Ladies Memorial Association of Wake County decided to decorate these Confederate graves on the anniversary of Gen. Thomas J. "Stonewall" Jackson's death, May 10, 1867. The city was still under martial law at the time, so no public recognition of the day was permitted.

When federal officers learned of the women's intentions, the ladies were told they would be fired upon if they formed a procession to the cemetery. In a classic act of passive resistance, they went to the graves in small groups of two or three, accompanied by federal officers who made sure no procession occurred. In 1936 the United Daughters of the Confederacy erected a House of Memory here in honor of the Confederate dead. Adjacent to Oakwood Cemetery is the Hebrew Cemetery, which contains a memorial to Jewish soldiers killed in military conflicts.

Return to the intersection of Bloodworth Street and Oakwood Avenue after touring the cemetery and turn right onto Bloodworth.

At number 411 is the Strong-Stronach House. The flags flying in front of the house mark the entrance to the Oakwood Inn Bed and Breakfast, also on the National Register of Historic Places. The white house with the one-level turrets just up the street at number 414 is the Upchurch-Stronach House. The turrets and the rosette window are distinctive Queen Anne features.

►Turn left onto Polk Street. The dark gray house on the corner at number 325 is the Judge Walter Clark House. Clark, chief justice of the North Carolina Supreme Court from 1903 to 1924, built this Queen Anne–style house for his mother and two sisters. Note the pink, white, and gray sunburst ornament in the front porch gable.

Number 318 is the Walter B. Barrow House. The wrap-around porch and the leaded glass front door are distinctive features of this house.

►Turn right onto Person Street. At the intersection of Pell and Person Streets is a sign for Peace College, which is to the left. You will see the grounds of Peace College on the return down Blount Street, so continue along Person Street.

Krispy Kreme Doughnut shop on the left at 549 Person Street is a good place to stop, rest, and get coffee and Krispy Kreme Doughnuts, a local tradition and a popular North Carolina product. The shop is open twenty-four hours a day, seven days a week, closed only on Christmas Day.

At the intersection of Person and Boundary Streets, look to the right at the fluted Ionic columns of the house at number 318. This is the Ellen Mordecai House; Ellen was the daughter of Moses Mordecai.

You are entering a shopping area with a pharmacy, post office, and other small shops. The sidewalk curves to the right and Person Street becomes Wake Forest Road. A sign in the center of the street welcomes you to the Mordecai community. Past the sign, you will see the border of Mordecai Historic Park on the opposite side of Wake Forest Road. Stay on Wake Forest Road, because you cannot cross here.

➤Turn left onto Chestnut Street.

➤Turn left onto Mordecai Drive.

➤Turn left onto Cedar Street, and in the middle of this block you will be able to enter the grounds of Mordecai Historic Park on your right.

The Mordecai House is the cream-colored structure with forest green shutters. If you are walking during hours of operation, you can purchase tickets to enter the house. If you are visiting during hours when the plantation house is closed, you may want to tour the grounds.

It is difficult to believe that in the early 1800s when the Mordecai family was at its peak of power and influence, a trip to the Mordecai plantation from downtown Raleigh was a trip to the country. The Mordecai family's land holdings covered much of what is now north Raleigh. On Sundays, downtown Raleigh residents took carriage rides 1 mile past the city limits at North Street, through cotton, corn, and wheat fields to the rural Mordecai plantation. Much of the woods and fields they saw on their journey were Mordecai holdings.

Today, Capital Area Preservation, Inc. maintains a park on the grounds of what was then the Mordecai plantation. The park includes structures original to the plantation that have survived the years. It also contains some structures, including Andrew Johnson's birthplace, that have been relocated to this park and arranged to create a replica of a nineteenth-century village street.

President Andrew Johnson's birthplace as seen from the garden at Mordecai Park.

The original part of the plantation house is the northern portion, built about 1785 by Joel Lane for his son Henry. When lawyer and farmer Moses Mordecai married into the family, it became known as the Mordecai House. Many of the interior furnishings are originals and provide an accurate picture of life in the antebellum South. Two original buildings now serve as the gift shop and a storage barn. A neoclassical Raleigh office building, which may have been Raleigh's post office in the mid-1900s, was transferred to the park in 1972 and houses Capital Area Preservation, Inc.

The Ellen Mordecai garden is a replica of a nineteenth-century garden and is open to the public during daylight hours.

An 1842 kitchen called the Allen kitchen was moved to what is believed to have been the site of the original Mordecai kitchen. Named for Mary Allen Huntley, the kitchen was moved from its original site in Wadesboro, North Carolina, to Raleigh in 1954 when the Huntley children donated it to the North Carolina Department of Archives. Accepted as a memorial to Mary, the kitchen was moved to its present location in 1968.

The birthplace of the seventeenth U.S. president, Andrew Johnson, was relocated to this park in 1975. Its original location was near an inn owned by Peter Casso near the corner of Raleigh's Fayetteville and Morgan Streets.

➤After touring the grounds of Mordecai Historic Park, walk behind the plantation house, following the driveway out to the street, and turn left onto Mordecai Drive.

➤Turn right onto Delway Street.

➤Turn left onto Blount Street.

Birth of a President

Peter Casso purchased land at the intersection of Morgan and Fayetteville Streets for $292 in 1795 and established an inn there. Two of his employees, Mary McDonough Johnson and Jacob Johnson, lived in one of the small houses on the premises of Casso's inn. On December 29, 1808, their second son Andrew (nicknamed Andy) was born.

Andy's father was an outgoing, popular man who often went hunting and fishing with Raleigh businessmen. When Andy was only three, Jacob died, possibly from complications after he jumped into nearby Walnut Creek to save two fishing companions.

Jacob was later recognized with a monument in the city cemetery for his bravery, but his death left his widow and two young sons financially strapped. Mary, unable to adequately provide for the boys, apprenticed them to tradesmen when they became fourteen. Andy was apprenticed to a tailor, and it was in the tailor's shop in spare moments that a shop foreman taught him to read and write. Life for an apprentice was hard and seemingly endless. This must have been true for Andy, because he ran away.

He later returned voluntarily to his master, but running away was a serious offense that marred his reputation. So his mother and her new husband moved to Tennessee to help Andy start over. There he married, made his living as a tailor, and became involved in politics, eventually becoming the president of the United States.

The house you see here is the original house, 12 by 18 feet. For years after Johnson became president, it was a popular tourist spot. Military men especially wanted to see the site of his birth and were always surprised at how tiny it was. It remains a popular attraction.

Walk 4

Peace College is to your right. More than 500 students graduate annually from this women's college. Peace is also notable because in 1879 the first kindergarten in the South was established here. If you wish to see more of Peace College, enter the campus at the Pace Street entrance. Return to Blount Street to resume the walk. Continue down the street; the second house on the left is the William Thomas House Bed and Breakfast, where you began the walk.

Walk 5
Gardens and Shopping

General location: Just west of the downtown Raleigh area.

Special attractions: Pullen Park, Raleigh Little Theater and Rose Garden, Cameron Village shopping center, a walk on a segment of Raleigh's famous greenway, the Jaycee Daylily Garden, and Cameron Park and Glenwood, two established neighborhoods known for their gardens and yards.

Difficulty rating: Mostly sidewalk; the Rose Garden and the Gardner Street Greenway portion are flat, dirt trails. Some slight hills.

Distance: 6.25 miles.

Walk 5

Estimated time: 3.25 hours.

Services: Restaurants on Hillsborough Street, in Cameron Village, and on Glenwood Avenue; restrooms in restaurants when open and at the Jaycee Park; picnicking, water, and restrooms at Jaycee Park and at Gardner Street Minipark; parking at Pullen Park, where the walk begins.

Note: Restrooms at parks are open limited hours.

Restrictions: Dogs must be leashed and droppings picked up. Avoid the Gardner Street Greenway during periods before, during, or after heavy rains, when flooding can occur. The greenway is not lighted; nighttime use is discouraged. The Raleigh Little Theater box office is open daily; contact the box office for schedules and prices.

For more information: Contact the Raleigh Department of Parks and Recreation, the Raleigh Little Theater, or the Capital Area Visitors Center.

Getting started: From I–440, take exit 2A, Western Boulevard, going east toward downtown Raleigh. You will pass North Carolina State University campus buildings on your right and left. After approximately 2 miles, turn left onto Ashe Avenue. The park is on the left. Park in the lot where you see the sign for Pullen Park.

Public transportation: Capital Area Transportation (CAT) bus 11 goes to Pullen Park Monday through Saturday. Contact CAT for information about times, fares, and accessibility.

Overview: This walk wanders through old Raleigh neighborhoods, Raleigh's most popular park with its unique carousel, several gardens, and one of Raleigh's preeminent shopping areas.

Gardens and Shopping

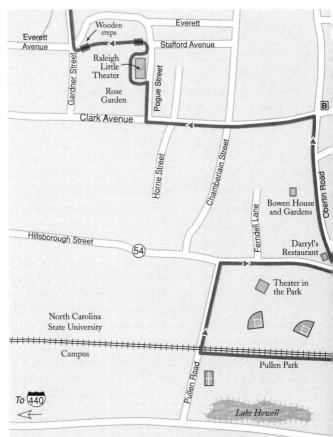

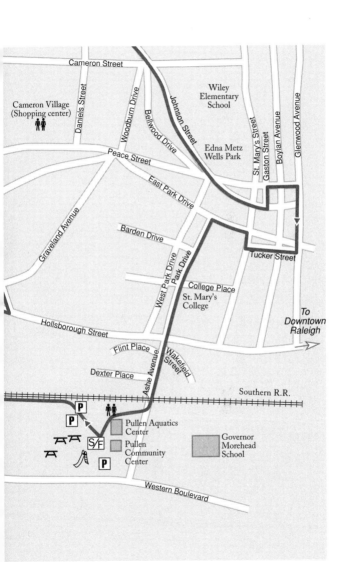

Gardens and Shopping

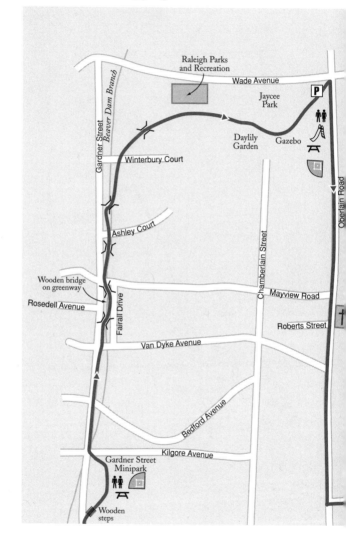

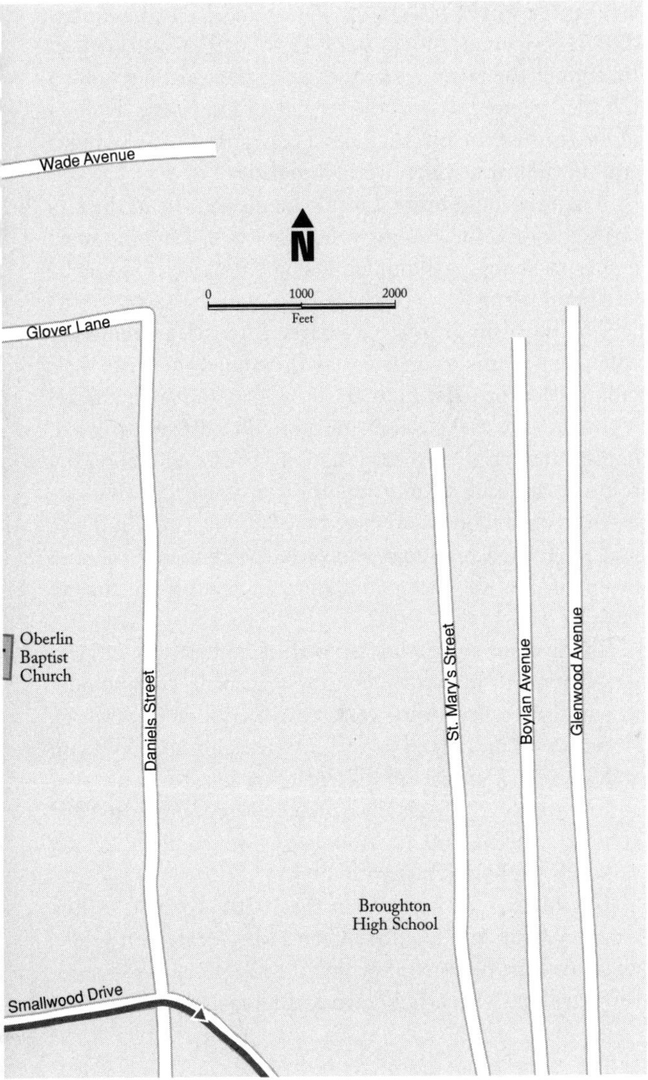

Wade Avenue
N
0
1000
2000
Feet
Glover Lane
Oberlin
Baptist
Church
Daniels Street
St. Mary's Street
Boylan Avenue
Glenwood Avenue
Broughton
High School
Smallwood Drive

On July 4, 1912, Carolina Power and Light Company (CP&L) opened Bloomsbury Park on the outskirts of Raleigh at the terminus of the city's streetcar lines, which CP&L operated. It was the heyday of electricity. To promote the use of electricity, CP&L strung 8,000 bulbs around the park, which were lit nightly.

A family could bring a picnic lunch and spend the day boating, riding the exciting roller coaster, or listening to an orchestra at the pavilion, while enjoying a treat from the ice cream parlor.

The most fun, however, was the carousel. Imagine the wide eyes of the youngsters as they lined up with their moms, dads, or older brothers and sisters to pay the nickel it cost to ride the carousel. Imagine little fingers crossed, hoping and wishing to ride on their favorite animal on the colorful carousel: twenty-nine horses, four pigs, four ostriches, four rabbits, four cats, two chariots, two giraffes, a lion, a tiger, a deer, a goat, and a mule were there to choose from—if one was lucky enough to be among the first in line.

Today children still line up with older brothers and sisters, parents or grandparents to wait in wide-eyed wonder to pay their seventy-five cents to ride the same carousel. Now located in Pullen Park, the carousel, made by William and Gustav Dentzel of Philadelphia, has been restored and refurbished. Originally purchased by CP&L in 1912 at a cost of $1,200, it is one of twenty-five Dentzel carousels surviving in this country.

Bloomsbury Park closed in the 1920s. Today Carolina Country Club and Country Club Hills, located on Glenwood Avenue between downtown Raleigh and I–440, occupy the land formerly known as Bloomsbury Park.

The Walk

➤The walk begins in the Pullen Park parking lot off Ashe Avenue.

➤Walk out of the parking lot, left of the community center between the playgrounds and tot lot. Stay on the sidewalk. At the top of the hill you will see a picnic gazebo on your left and a newer wooden picnic shelter on your right. Parking lots are located on the right and the left of the park access road before the road widens into another parking lot and ends.

➤In the cul-de-sac, take the sidewalk to the left. Only pedestrian traffic is permitted in this part of the park.

Pullen Park is a large, heavily used urban park with many amenities, some free and some for a fee. Picnic tables grace the wide lawns of the park. The park contains the Dentzel carousel, kiddie boats, pedal boats, a miniature train, concessions, aquatic center, an arts center, and at 107 Pullen Road, the state's largest community theater. Mature oaks, maples, and pines, among other trees, cover the park.

➤At the end of the sidewalk, turn right onto Pullen Road. Look right while crossing the bridge that passes over the railroad tracks for a good view of the downtown Raleigh skyline. Part of the North Carolina State University campus is on the left just beyond the railroad tracks, and more of Pullen Park is on the right. This portion of Pullen Park contains ballparks and Pullen Theater.

➤Walk between the brick columns that mark the Hillsborough Street entrance to Pullen Park, and turn right, walking down Hillsborough Street.

You can stop for coffee, lunch, or dinner at number 1906, Darryl's 1906 Restaurant, a famous Raleigh landmark.

➤ Cross Hillsborough Street to your left at the pedestrian crosswalk just beyond Darryl's; Hillsborough is a busy Raleigh street, so take care as you cross. A sign directs you to Cameron Village at this intersection of Oberlin Road and Hillsborough Street. You are now on the sidewalk adjacent to Oberlin Road.

Along this portion of Oberlin Road, you will see North Carolina State University campus buildings, including the

Of Interest

The Isabel Bowen Henderson House and Gardens

At the ivy-covered trees and chain-link fence at 213 Oberlin Road, note the engraving in the sidewalk. The Henderson House and Garden is listed on the National Register of Historic Places. A wall plaque reads, THE IS-ABELLE BOWEN HENDERSON HOUSE AND GARDENS. Born in Raleigh in 1899, Bowen was a teacher, gardener, portrait painter, and craftswoman. Her portraitures hang in the collection at the North Carolina Museum of Art, and in the state supreme court. She was a founder and life-long member of the North Carolina Museum of Art. Her gardening skills won her the 1951 National Horticultural Award, and she was famous for her 600 varieties of iris and more than 500 varieties of *Hemerocallis*.

The Williamsburg revival house and gardens you see here are owned by Bowen family members. They were placed on the National Register of Historic Places in 1989 and on the list of Raleigh Historic Properties, partly to protect them from construction of a freeway.

Center for Universal Design at 219 Oberlin Road. On the right are the shops of Cameron Village.

▶Turn left onto Clark Avenue. You are walking past several homes and businesses. Just past Fairmont Methodist Church at the top of the small hill is a sign directing you to the Raleigh Little Theater and Rose Garden.

▶Turn right onto Pogue Street. Take care as you cross Clark Avenue's three lanes.

Of Interest

The Raleigh Little Theater, Amphitheater, and Rose Garden

Now a Raleigh Historic Property, the Raleigh Little Theater, with its clear, simple, straight lines, was founded in 1939 on the site of the state fair race track. Born in the Great Depression and sponsored by the Works Progess Administration, the entire project was a community effort. Plants were donated by nurseries and garden clubs, and merchants gave materials and equipment.

The theater is adjacent to a 3,000-seat amphitheater and a rose garden. The rose garden was added in 1948, when 3,000 rose bushes were planted. A semicircular arbor, approximately 150 feet long and built on stone columns, is adorned with climbing roses and wisteria. The arbor, along with the vast beds of roses making up the sunken garden, combine to make this a rose lover's dream in the summer when the fragrance of roses fills the air.

It is also a popular place for celebration. In the warm months you will likely be walking around a wedding party. Other groups hold parties in the amphitheater and the sunken rose garden.

➤Turn left at Stafford Street and cross Pogue Street. The Raleigh Little Theater is on the left at number 301.

➤Walk past the main doors and onto the balcony for a good view of the rose garden.

➤Walk down the stairs from the balcony in the rear of the theater building that lead to the office.

➤Continue walking past the office and up toward Pogue Street.

➤Turn left at the fire hydrant; immediately turn left, and follow the stone steps flanked by wooden railings down into the sunken rose garden. These steps can be slick during rainy weather, so descend carefully. The steps end at a dirt path leading to the arbor.

➤Turn right and walk under the arbor. Look left for good views of the rose garden, and rest on a bench under the arbor. As you rest, you may enjoy the sights and sounds of a celebration under way in the garden or at the amphitheater.

➤At the end of the arbor, turn right, and walk up the flight of wooden steps.

➤At the top of the steps, turn right onto Gardner Street.

➤Follow the set of wooden steps into Gardner Street Minipark at 1412 Gardner Street. This small, urban neighborhood park contains a ball field, picnic tables, playground, water fountain, and restrooms.

➤Follow the sidewalk through the park.

➤Turn left at the end of the sidewalk and go to the next intersection, which is not signed. You will see a fire hydrant and a sign with a directional arrow pointing to the Jaycee Park. Look for the hydrant and the directional sign for Jaycee Park to help you at these intersections because there are no street signs. You are now walking on a sidewalk along Gardner Street.

►Turn right onto Van Dyke Avenue at the intersection with Gardner Street. You will see another sign for the Jaycee Park, which is approximately 0.5 mile ahead on the greenway.

►Turn left onto Fairall Drive, an unpaved street. You will now see signs marking the Capital Area Greenway. Gardner Street is to your left. Along this portion of the greenway, you are walking in a forest by Beaver Dam Branch. You are also walking along the rear of a residential neighborhood and adjacent to residential backyards.

►At the stop sign on Mayview Road, turn left, cross at the pedestrian crosswalk, and walk on the sidewalk along Gardner Street. In the middle of the block and just before you reach Ashley Court, look right and you will see a wooden footbridge.

►Cross the footbridge. The greenway runs beside the street on a footpath.

►Veer to the left, following the path through the thick undergrowth.

The vegetation consists of large poplars, oaks, and pines. Undergrowth includes many vines, plants, small bushes, young trees, and ivy. Watch for poison ivy.

You will begin to hear traffic noise, which at times you had left completely as you walked through this dense forest.

►Walk downhill and cross another footbridge. This is a steep downgrade, so watch your footing. Walk through the grassy area uphill toward the brick building housing the Raleigh Parks and Recreation office. If it is open, you can pick up park and greenway maps. You are now at the end of the Gardner Street Greenway.

➤When you reach the pavement, turn right and follow the brick paths as they wander through the Jaycee Daylily Garden. Daylilies bloom in June and July. If you are in Raleigh during the summer months, you will enjoy the many colors of the more than one hundred species of lilies in this garden. Walk toward the gazebo, where you can stop, rest, and enjoy the garden.

➤Follow the path up and to the left of the gazebo out of the garden. Follow the sidewalk to the parking lot. A playground, ball fields, picnic area, and restrooms are located here.

➤When you are ready to leave the park and garden, cross the parking lot and head toward Wade Avenue, the street in front of Jaycee Park. The sidewalk resumes between the parking lot and Wade Avenue at the upper end of the parking lot. The sidewalk veers away from the drive bordering Jaycee Park and goes up a slight hill to Oberlin Road.

➤When you reach the stop sign and yield sign, veer to the right onto Oberlin Road. At 1012 Oberlin Road, you will see the YWCA. A small community grocery, the Community Deli, on the right at number 901, is a convenient place to purchase sandwiches, soft drinks, and other snacks.

➤Cross the road at the pedestrian crosswalk in front of Oberlin Baptist Church at the intersection of Oberlin Road and Roberts Avenue. You are now following the sidewalk on the left side of Oberlin Road and entering a commercial area of shops and banks that surround Cameron Village.

Children of all ages enjoy the carousel at Pullen Park. (Courtesy Peter Damroth/Greater Raleigh Convention and Visitors Bureau)

➤Turn left onto Smallwood Drive. Along this street, you will have several opportunities to enter Cameron Village, where you will find shopping, several restaurants, bakeries, a grocery, coffee shops, and more.

Built on land from the Duncan Cameron estate, this shopping center first opened in 1949, making it the earliest regional shopping center in the Southeast and one of the first in the United States. Smallwood Drive is named for the Smallwoods, one of whom married a Cameron. Originally the shopping center was to have been named Smallwood Village.

Along Smallwood Drive you will be walking through residential neighborhoods, many of them carved from Cameron land when the land was sold. Among the properties originally owned by the Camerons was the land where Raleigh Apartments now stand. Note signs for Broughton High School, also originally part of the Cameron estate.

At the intersection with Peace Street, use the pedestrian traffic push button signal to help you cross this busy street.

➤Smallwood Drive becomes Johnson Street. Edna Metz Wells Park is on the left as you walk up one way Johnson Street. In this small park you will find picnic tables as well as benches.

You are on the outskirts of Cameron Park, one of Raleigh's showcase neighborhoods. You will have the opportunity to see more of the houses and gardens of Cameron Park later in the walk. Take time now to notice the beautiful gardens and lawns of the houses along Johnson Street.

➤Turn left onto Gaston Street. You are now entering the Glenwood neighborhood, an old residential neighborhood being revitalized and fast becoming a popular Raleigh

Boating and picnicking are popular activities at Pullen Park. (Courtesy Peter Damroth/Greater Raleigh Convention and Visitors Bureau)

business and residential area. Older homes are being remodeled or turned into galleries, boutiques, and gourmet restaurants along side streets in Glenwood as well as on Glenwood Avenue.

➤Turn right onto Peace Street.

➤Turn right onto Glenwood Avenue. Stop and sample some of the good food and beverage at any of the restaurants along the avenue, including the Steel Porcupine and Moonlight Pizza.

➤Turn right onto Tucker Street.

➤Turn right onto St. Mary's Street.

➤Turn left onto East Park Drive.

Of Interest

Cameron Park: The Gardening Neighborhood

Cameron Park has been nicknamed the Neighborhood That Gardens and has been featured in several magazines for its beautiful, often distinctive gardens. One house features an English cottage garden; the next boasts a rock garden; another has a formal garden; and at least one has a bonsai garden. Herb gardens are also very popular.

The homes themselves are distinctive and offer a wide variety of architecture to enjoy. You will probably want to linger along this road, even wandering up some of the side streets or alleys to get closer looks at backyards and side yard gardens, especially if you are walking in the summer or in a holiday season.

➤Turn left onto Park Drive.

On your left at the intersection of College Place and Park Drive are the grounds of St. Mary's College, an Episcopal preparatory school.

➤At the top of the incline, cross Hillsborough Street. When you cross the street, you will follow Ashe Avenue, which runs through a small residential neighborhood adjacent to Pullen Park. Despite the smaller houses and less spectacular gardens, the gardening craze continues on this side of Hillsborough Street. Be sure to notice the bamboo fencing and garden in the yard of the house at number 119.

Governor Morehead School on the left was formerly known as the North Carolina School for the Blind. On the right, is a sign for Pullen Park Community Center.

➤Turn right into this parking lot, which is where you end this walk.

Walk 6
Wolfpack Walk

General location: The heart of the main campus of North Carolina State University (NCSU).

Special attractions: Memorial Bell Tower, Carmichael Gymnasium, D. H. Hill Library, Reynolds Coliseum, NCSU bookstores, University Student Center, Derr Track, and other campus buildings.

Difficulty rating: Easy, mostly flat, some hills that will be moderate for those in wheelchairs. Surface is cement, asphalt, and brick sidewalk. The brick sidewalk is uneven in places. A square sticker is placed on all wheelchair-accessible doors. There is no direct wheelchair-accessible route between north and south campuses; directions for an alternate route between these two campuses are included in the text at the point where you enter the Free Expression Tunnel.

Wolfpack Walk

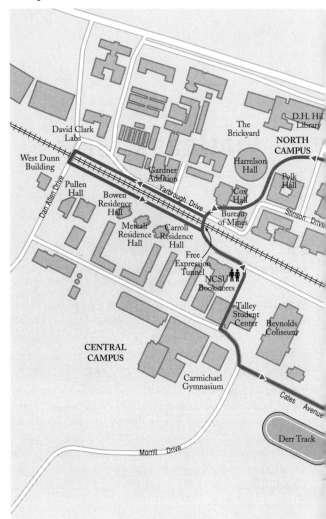

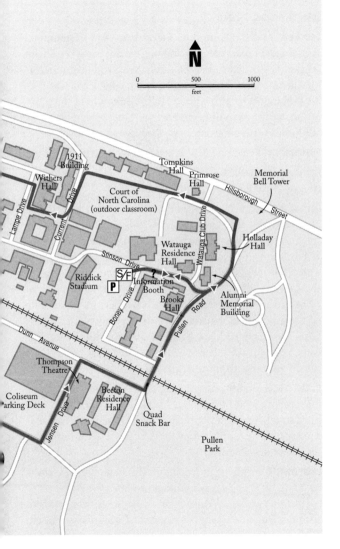

Distance: 2 miles.

Estimated time: 1 hour.

Services: Food at campus snack bars and restaurants. Restrooms in most campus buildings; many are wheelchair-accessible. To determine a building's accessibility, look for blue arrows placed on the wall of each wheelchair-accessible building. The arrow points in the direction of the nearest accessible entrance. Emergency blue light telephones are located at regular intervals throughout campus.

Restrictions: Pets must be leashed and droppings picked up.

For more information: Contact NCSU University Information or Disability Services for Students.

Getting started: From I–40, take Hillsborough Street, exit 290, which is also known as NC 54, east toward downtown Raleigh. Approximately 1 mile past the overpass for I–440, you will begin to see university signs and buildings. Turn right onto Pullen Road, which is the road just after the Memorial Bell Tower. Turn right onto the campus on Stinson Drive. The information booth sits in the middle of Stinson Drive; you can pick up a visitor parking pass here. To reach Riddick Stadium parking lot where this walk begins, turn left onto Boney Drive just beyond the information booth on the right.

Public transportation: All four lines of Wolfline, the campus bus system, stop on Stinson Drive. NCSU is also served by Capital Area Transit (CAT) and Triangle Transit Authority (TTA). Contact Wolfline, CAT, or TTA for times, fares, and accessibility.

Overview: The largest university in the state, North Carolina State University was founded in 1887.

If you walked Walk 5 in this book, you walked through Pullen Park. It is named for R. Stanhope Pullen, who donated the land that eventually became the park. Adjacent to that property is another sixty-two-acre tract once owned by Pullen. He donated this land for the college known today as North Carolina State University, but originally it was known as North Carolina College of Agriculture and Mechanic Arts. Leading a mule pulling a plow, Pullen divided the land given to the city and the property given to the college. To this day, Pullen Road divides the park and the east border of the campus along the furrow Pullen plowed.

Other facets of college life have changed. The first class in 1889 had seventy-two students; today enrollment exceeds 24,000. The first students carried a bucket to a well to draw their water; today NCSU is a leader in technology and research, among other fields. Pullen's original 62 acres are still in use by NCSU, along with other property totaling 623 acres on the main campus alone. Holladay Hall, which you will pass on this walk, was the original building on the campus. In fact, it was the only building for years, with faculty offices, student and faculty dining, a chapel, classrooms, and barracks upstairs for the seventy-two students housed within its walls. Holladay Hall is one of one hundred fifty buildings on the main campus.

A significant part of life for thousands of NCSU students, as well as NCSU fans everywhere, is sports, chiefly basketball and football. The Wolfpack, for whom this walk is named, is a proud symbol for many alumni. NCSU basketball is a national as well as a state treasure, and if you are one of the many Wolfpack fans, alumni or not, you will especially enjoy this walk through the red and white territory of the Wolfpack.

If large urban universities intrigue you, yet you find it difficult to get a grasp on their campuses, this walk is for you.

The Walk

Note: The Triangle Trailblazers, a local walking club, collected information about the Memorial Bell Tower and part of the walk on campus; some of their comments are used here.

➤When you exit the Riddick Stadium parking lot, turn right onto Stinson Drive.

To locate Stinson Drive from the parking lot, stand so that stadium seating is on your left in the parking area. Look right, and you will see a set of brick steps leading up and out of the parking lot on the northeast end of the lot. Take these steps. If you are in a wheelchair or pushing a stroller, exit the parking lot onto Boney Drive, the side street on the right of the parking lot. At the end of Boney Drive, you will be on Stinson Drive.

➤Walk past the information booth where you picked up your parking pass. Those in wheelchairs will find this hill to be steep, so take your time. You are walking on brick sidewalk; much of NCSU is paved in red brick. The Watauga Residence Hall is on your left at the intersection of Stinson Drive and Watauga Club Drive.

➤Turn left onto Pullen Road. The Alumni Memorial Building is to your left.

Holladay Hall, the next building on your left, was named for NCSU's first president, Alexander Quarles Holladay; this imposing structure was for many years the only academic structure on campus.

Memorial Bell Tower, or the bell tower, as it is popularly known, is just ahead between Holladay Hall and Hillsborough Street. Built in 1919, the tower is a famous Raleigh landmark and North Carolina state landmark. Dedicated by the alumni association and built by the

Walk 6

Works Progress Administration, the tower honors thirty-three NCSU students killed in World War I. The bell tower's base is wheelchair-accessible.

►When you leave the bell tower, walk away from Pullen Road and Hillsborough Street toward Watauga Club Drive.

►Cross Watauga Club Drive. Primrose Hall is on your right. Notice the waterfall to your right in the center of a small shaded courtyard, a monument dedicated to the class of 1914.

You should now be on the large, grassy area in front of Tompkins Hall known as the Court of North Carolina. This lawn, popular with students for relaxing, studying, socializing, and sunbathing, was dedicated at the beginning of the university's centennial year to the faculty and students of past, present, and future generations. If classes are in session as you walk, you may even see a class being conducted in the outdoor classroom located on the Court.

►Walk through the courtyard, either on the brick sidewalk or along the brick courtyard under the river birches. Benches provide places to rest.

►As you walk through the courtyard, veer right until you arrive at Current Drive. Part of this is a steep grade for those in wheelchairs.

►Turn left onto Current Drive. Notice the large, white brick columns of the 1911 Building on your right; a snack bar is in this building. Names of fraternities are set in stone in the sidewalk in front of the holly trees to your left.

►Turn right at the pedestrian crosswalk at the end of this building. Stairs and a ramp provide access here.

►At the top of the ramp, use either the stairs or sidewalk to turn right. Withers Hall is on your right.

➤Cross Lampe Drive in front of Withers Hall using the pedestrian crosswalk. Walk past the brick columns into Gardner Arboretum, a small, quiet oasis of native plants near the middle of North Campus.

Directly ahead you will see a famous NCSU landmark: the statue of the strolling professor. Dressed in a suit and holding a book in his right hand, he is reading as he walks; from a distance he looks real. Notice the leather-looking bookmark in his book.

➤In front of the statue, bear right and continue west to another NCSU landmark, University Plaza, better known as the Brickyard. D. H. Hill Library, a 1.5-million-volume library, is on your right.

On the grassy area before you enter the Brickyard, look for the Listening Vessels, a large, tan, disk-shaped column. Then find the second column about 90 feet away from and in front of the first one. If you are walking with a partner, try experimenting with the Listening Vessels by doing the following: One of you take a seat in one column; the other take a seat in the second column. Even though you are about 90 feet apart and on a noisy, heavily used pedestrian plaza, when you talk to each other in a normal tone of voice, you will be able to hear each other perfectly.

The Brickyard is just that: a yard paved in red bricks interspersed with white brick in an attractive geometric design. It is the site of many NCSU pep rallies and is the central gathering place on North Campus.

Look for Harrelson Hall, the round building surrounded by pines and dogwoods on the lower side of the Brickyard.

NCSU's statue of The Strolling Professor *looks life-like.*

➤Walk left of Harrelson Hall so that you are between Harrelson and Polk Halls. This is the best access for those in wheelchairs.

➤Turn right between Cox Hall and the Bureau of Mines. The Free Expression Tunnel, the tunnel that connects North and South Campuses and that runs under the Southern Railroad tracks, is ahead. Take the steps down into the tunnel.

When you see the tunnel you will immediately understand its name. Graffiti covers every available surface: walls, ceilings, floors, and light fixtures.

➤Stay to the right as you go through the tunnel; this busy pedestrian thoroughfare is one of three pedestrian tunnels connecting the two campuses.

Note: Wheelchair users, the Free Expression Tunnel is not accessible. To reach the South Campus, go under the arch along the brick sidewalk to Yarbrough Drive. Turn right and pass the Gardner Addition Building. You will also pass some greenhouses to your right. When you reach Dan Allen Drive, turn left in front of David Clark Labs. West Dunn Building should be to your right and you should be in front of Pullen Hall. Turn left again, leaving Dan Allen Drive, passing through the campus. You will be passing by several residence halls, including Bowen, Metcalf, and Carroll, and back to the Free Expression Tunnel's south entrance.

➤In front of the southern entrance to the tunnel, turn left. Those in wheelchairs, this is where you pick up the walk again.

The building with the columns and the geometric roofline just ahead and to the right is the bookstore. Visitors are welcome in the bookstore. Here you can choose from a wide selection of gifts, many with the Wolfpack logo, as well as textbooks, other books, and office supplies. The bookstore also has a restaurant and restrooms.

➤When you exit the bookstore where you entered, turn right. Look for the ramp to the right bordered by white cement walls and a fountain to the left. This is the entrance to the University Student Center.

➤Turn right and walk along this ramp with the white cement walls. The fountain should be to your left. Enter the University Student Center, where you will find refreshments, restrooms, the information center, Stewart Theater, and schedules of campus events, among other services. You can purchase tickets to campus events here. Be sure to try the ice cream in the convenience store; it is a product of NCSU's dairy plants.

➤When you are ready to leave the student center, walk out the back entrance. You will be facing Carmichael Gymnasium when you exit the center.

Visitors are welcome in Carmichael Gymnasium; you can purchase individual passes in the gymnasium office. The gym offers a fitness center, two Olympic-size swimming pools, basketball courts, indoor tennis, indoor track, racquetball, volleyball, badminton, weight rooms, a sauna, and an aerobics studio. If you go inside, be sure to see Mount Wolfpack, an indoor rock wall, which offers rock climbing and rappelling.

➤Face the gymnasium, and turn left. At the intersection of Cates Avenue and Morrill Drive, cross Morrill Drive, so you are following Cates Avenue. This is a busy campus intersection, so use the pedestrian crossings.

The Reynolds Coliseum south entrance is on the left. Wheelchair-accessible entrances to the coliseum are available, should you wish to enter. Look for the ramps. Reynolds Coliseum is the home of Wolfpack basketball and is a popular place on campus for dances, bands, and orchestras. The coliseum is home to the campus ROTC program.

➤Return to this intersection after visiting the coliseum and turn left, continuing down Cates Avenue. Paul Derr track is on your right.

➤Turn left onto Jensen Drive. The Thompson Theatre is on your right, and the coliseum parking deck is on your left.

➤Turn right onto Dunn Avenue. Becton Residence Hall and the Quad Snack Bar are on the right.

➤Turn left so that you are walking along Pullen Road. You have now left the brick sidewalk and are on paved sidewalk, which is asphalt for a short distance and then becomes concrete. Pullen Park is on your right across Pullen Road. You will cross the overpass over Southern Railroad. Look right for a good view of the Raleigh skyline.

➤Just past Brooks Hall School of Design, look for the steps or follow the sidewalk to turn left onto Stinson Drive. You will see the sign just ahead for visitor parking and information, where you began this walk.

Walk 7
JC Raulston Arboretum

General location: The JC Raulston Arboretum at North Carolina State University.

Special attractions: The Klein-Pringle White Garden, nandina collection, magnolia collection, water gardens, rose garden, Japanese gardens, and Paradise Garden.

Difficulty rating: Easy, flat, mostly grass surface. Wooden boardwalk in some places; stone and brick sidewalks in the specialty gardens.

Distance: 0.5 mile.

Estimated time: 30 minutes.

Services: Restrooms are available.

Restrictions: Open 8:00 A.M. to dusk daily. No pets. Do not remove plants.

JC Raulston Arboretum

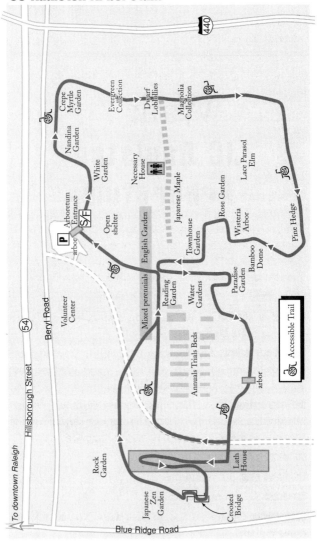

Those in wheelchairs should be aware that since much of the walk is on grassy surfaces, it could be difficult to navigate a wheelchair if the ground is very wet.

For more information: Contact the JC Raulston Arboretum. Visitor and volunteer information is located in the brick building across from the visitor parking lot.

Getting started: To reach the arboretum from I–440, take exit 3, Hillsborough Street (NC 54), west. Turn left onto Blue Ridge Road, and almost immediately turn left onto Beryl Road. You will see signs for the arboretum, which is on the right. Turn onto the graveled driveway; parking is available here.

Public transportation: None.

Overview: "Plan and plant for a better world" was Dr. JC Raulston's motto, one that he lived by. Through the arboretum named for him, he has provided many others with the means to follow this maxim. In 1976 Dr. Raulston, a horticultural science professor at North Carolina State University, began working with students, plant industry professionals, and others to create a garden to discover and promote new plants. He began traveling and collecting plants from all over the world, many of which he eventually used in his campus garden.

After his death in a car accident in 1996 at the age of fifty-six, the garden was renamed the JC Raulston Arboretum in his honor. It continues to grow, and his work is being carried on by others who have followed him, including students, volunteers, and plant professionals.

The arboretum's eight acres contain approximately 6,000 different plant varieties from fifty-five countries. More than 100,000 visitors stroll the gardens annually to enjoy its serenity, to get ideas for home gardens, or, in the case of plant professionals, to choose the plants they will sell in their businesses.

Although some exhibits in the arboretum are permanent, it is a dynamic garden, changing regularly. The exhibits you see one month may not necessarily be the ones you see the next month or the next season. This variety fits in well with the research, educational, and outreach purposes of the arboretum. The garden serves as a laboratory for graduate and undergraduate students as well as a place where the general public and plant industry professionals can see which plants grow best in the Southeast.

This walk takes you through a small portion of these eight acres and provides an opportunity to view some of the highlights of the arboretum. However, after this short walk, you may find your appetite whetted for more of the gardens. Be sure to pick up a copy of the arboretum's map, so that when you spy something else that interests you, you can identify it.

Something is always blooming in the arboretum, even in the dead of winter. Any time you need or want to stop and rest, take advantage of the benches that have been generously placed in the gardens.

The Walk

Note: The arboretum is not static. As a classroom and laboratory, it constantly changes. The route described here has been established for some time; however, like all of the arboretum, it is subject to change. If the plants and gardens or walkways you find vary from the directions that follow, you will understand why.

➤From the visitor parking lot, walk under the arbor into the open shelter to begin the tour.

The colorful gardens at JC Raulston Arboretum provide a delightful place to stroll. (Courtesy Peter Damroth/Greater Raleigh Convention and Visitors Bureau)

➤From the open shelter, walk straight ahead.

The first garden in the arboretum is the Klein-Pringle White Garden, so named because the theme is white. All foliage has been selected for its white, silver, or gray color. The effect of this garden is very relaxing and calming because of its light, neutral colors.

➤Follow the brick and tile walkways for approximately 10 yards. At the end of the tile sidewalk, follow the grassy path through the nandina garden along the perimeter of the arboretum. As you leave the nandina garden, you will pass a small garden of fragrant ornamental cedars and a garden of crepe myrtle.

➤When you reach the chain-link fence serving as a boundary for the arboretum, turn right.

Here the lower side of the garden on both sides of the path is an evergreen collection that focuses on blue evergreens. Take a deep breath in this part of the garden and enjoy the scent of pine and evergreen. The texture and silvery blue color of these conifers make this area of the arboretum a year-round pleasure.

Approximately 100 feet ahead are the dwarf loblolly pines, unique to this arboretum. These pines have not been located anywhere else in the world, and staff members have been unable to propagate these unusual pines.

Just past the loblollies, the magnolia collection on both sides of the path contains several varieties of these trees, all of which have large, white fragrant flowers in late spring and early summer. In the arboretum in the magnolia garden are the restrooms, referred to as the Necessary House. Throughout the arboretum you can see the colorfully painted walls of the Necessary House, with the distinctive weather vane on the roof.

➤Go straight at the next intersection. In the wide-open space is a lace parasol elm, also known as a dwarf weeping elm. Continue following the perimeter of the garden, staying on the grassy trail. You can see a rose garden through a pine hedge.

➤At the next intersection, turn right, walking between a

bamboo dome on your left and a wisteria-covered arbor on your right.

➤Just past the wisteria arbor, follow the brick path.

➤Enter the rose garden, which contains a variety of roses; some are in bloom almost any season. Directly across the brick path in front of the rose garden is a marble sculpture, *Italian Architecture,* by Horace Farlowe, which honors Dr. Raulston.

➤Return along the brick path to the grassy path and continue your walk.

The first theme garden, the Townhouse Garden, contains a raised deck—a wonderful place to stop, rest, and savor the sights. A Japanese maple is in this garden. The symbol of the arboretum, Japanese maples are visible from any point in the arboretum.

Approximately 100 feet beyond the Townhouse Garden are the mixed perennials, better known as the English Garden. Depending on the time of year, you will enjoy the profusion of colorful plants of various heights spilling out of their borders. It is meant to be a regularly changing swath of colors, and in many seasons it lives up to this goal.

➤Turn back and retrace your steps through the theme gardens. The first theme garden, the Reading Garden, is a quiet, peaceful nook.

The second theme garden is the water gardens. Paved stones across the small goldfish pond invite you to cross and get a closer look at the goldfish swimming between and under the water lilies.

➤Enter the next garden, the Middle Eastern, or Paradise Garden, so called because Middle Easterners consider having a small garden like this one to be paradise. A circular tile mosaic depicting the four seasons is the focus of this garden.

➤When you exit the Paradise Garden, turn and walk back to the grassy trail you left to enter the rose garden.

➤Walk along the grassy trail by the perimeter of the arboretum and onto the stone sidewalk.

➤In approximately 100 feet, turn left of the grassy path onto the flagstone walkway. The walkway passes under an arbor about 30 feet ahead of you. Stand in the arbor, and look to your right at the annuals trials. Annuals are tested here each year to see how they perform, and nursery owners come to observe these annuals in bloom to help them determine which ones to take to market.

➤Follow the stone walkway through the arbor. Just ahead is a brick sidewalk that leads to a testing garden. About 400 plant varieties here allow you to test your ability to identify them.

➤When you leave the testing garden, return to this point, and walk approximately 20 feet. You are now walking alongside the lath house.

Note: For those in wheelchairs, this is the end of the accessible portion of the walk. To return to the starting point, follow the gravel road to the visitor parking area.

➤Enter the lath house, a slat-roof structure that reduces sun exposure by 15 percent. Plants in the lath house, such as hostas, azaleas, and ivy, prefer more shade.

➤Walk through the lath house. You will want to take your time and closely examine some of the many plants that make their home here. It is a good place to get ideas for your own home gardens, so you may even want to jot down the names of plants that interest you.

➤Exit the lath house, and notice on your immediate left a large clump of golden bamboo. This marks the entrance to the Japanese Garden. The stone path is rather uneven at this point, so take care. You will walk across what is known as the Crooked Bridge.

➤Continue to follow the stone path farther into this garden. You will see a rock garden ahead and a crepe myrtle with unusual coral bark. The Japanese Garden is designed to calm and create a meditative state. Take a seat in front of the "ocean and mountains" landscape and reflect on the serenity of this environment. The blue gravel represents the ocean, the brown vegetation represents the shore, and the taller trees the forests.

➤Exit the Japanese Garden, and walk beside the end of the lath house along a curving gravel path lined with concrete blocks.

➤Cross the gravel road.

➤Walk between the annual beds and the mixed perennial gardens.

➤Take the first left, which puts you between two tall hollies and onto a wide, tile walkway. Continue approximately 50 feet to the open shelter, where you began the walk.

Walk 8
Lake Johnson Trail

General location: Lake Johnson is located in southwest Raleigh just inside the I–440 beltline.

Special attractions: Lake Johnson, lakeshore walking with good views of the lake and wildlife.

Difficulty rating: Moderate, mostly flat, a few small hills; the walk is on a paved asphalt pedestrian trail. A wooden pedestrian bridge spans the lake near the end of the walk.

Distance: 3.5 miles.

Estimated time: 2 hours.

Services: Picnic tables and shelter. Boat and paddleboat rentals. Fishing and biking. Emergency phone boxes located along the trail. Water fountain at the boathouse.

Restrictions: Restrooms open only on weekends mid-March through mid-October, sunrise to sunset. No swimming or private boat launching. No alcoholic beverages,

Walk 8

Lake Johnson Trail

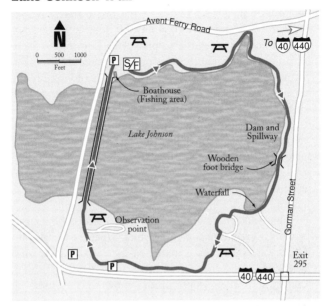

no firearms, no fires, no motorized vehicles except in designated places. Bring water on the walk. Pets must be leashed and droppings picked up. Because of some of the isolated areas of this walk, it is recommended that you walk with a partner.

For more information: Contact the City of Raleigh Department of Parks and Recreation.

Getting started: From I–40/440, take exit 295, Gorman Street, north. At approximately 1 mile, turn left onto Avent Ferry Road. The visitor parking area is near the boat ramp about 1 mile farther down 4501 Avent Ferry Road.

Public transportation: None.

Overview: Raleigh boasts one of the finest greenway systems in the country. With almost 30 miles in the current system and growing, the Capital Area Greenway system provides recreational facilities plus opportunities for thousands of people in the greater Raleigh area to sample the area's ecological features. The Capital Area Greenway is certainly a major reason Raleigh continually picks up national awards for its walking and outdoor recreational activities. The ultimate goal of the Capital Area Greenway program is to establish a closed network of interconnected trails so that a walker can navigate much of Raleigh and even walk beyond the city's boundaries via the greenway system.

This walk lets you sample the Lake Johnson Greenway, a popular greenway and park, which is part of the Walnut Creek Greenway. As a matter of fact, if you walk on a weekend, expect crowds; the picnic areas, boating, fishing, biking, and hiking opportunities entice many visitors on pretty weekend afternoons.

In spite of the potential crowds, when you walk along the greenway that encompasses Lake Johnson you can feel completely alone. The tall pines that surround the lake sway gently in the breeze that ripples the surface of the lake. You can look out on the lake from several vantage points along the trail and not see another soul.

If you enjoy picnicking, pack your lunch to take with you on this walk. Several areas on the trail provide scenic places to enjoy your meal.

The footbridge across Lake Johnson provides scenic lake views.

The Walk

➤The walk starts by the boathouse. From the boathouse parking lot on Avent Ferry Road, turn toward the Capital Area Greenway sign and walk through a forest of pines and hardwoods. Views of the lake are to your right.

Benches are provided along the trail so you can stop and enjoy the lake views. A residential neighborhood is on your left along this portion of the walk. At approximately 0.5 mile, you will see a picnic table in a setting overlooking the lake. Shortly, you will leave the residential neighborhood.

➤At 0.75 mile, cross the dam and spillway. The walk is level and easy, and you will have good lake views from the trail along the dam. Stop and enjoy the view and the pine forests surrounding the lake.

➤Cross the wooden footbridge just after you leave the dam and enter another wooded area.

At 1.25 miles, give yourself a break at the bench and enjoy the view. Take a deep breath and enjoy the fragrance of pine. Look right at the spillway and the footbridge you just crossed. You may see ducks on the lake or squirrels playing in the pine branches.

➤At the fork in the road ahead, go right.

The incline at 1.75 miles is the steepest part of the walk. Take your time and enjoy the sights as you ascend this hill. Look for the retaining wall that provides seating. Sit and look for the small waterfall.

➤At the next intersection, which is a circle, turn right and go downhill.

➤Go right at the next intersection.

A path leads to a picnic area and an observation point at the 2.5-mile point. In this area, the pine forest is interspersed with stands of bigleaf magnolia.

➤Stay on the trail. You will see several paved spurs to your left along this portion of the trail, all of which lead to a parking area.

➤At the foot of the hill, cross the long wooden pedestrian footbridge. Stop on the footbridge and look to your right at the lake you just circled. At the end of the footbridge, you are back at the boathouse where you began the walk.

Want to see more of Lake Johnson? Cross Avent Ferry Road at the boathouse. A 1-mile bark chip trail parallels the lakeshore and leads to Athens Drive High School on the northern side of Avent Ferry Road.

Walk 9
Shelley Lake Trail

General location: Shelley Lake is in northwest Raleigh south of and adjacent to Sertoma Arts Center, about 6 miles from downtown.

Special attractions: Shelley Lake, Sertoma Arts Center, fishing, boating, picnicking, playground, soccer and other field activities, lakeshore walking, good lake views, nature study.

Difficulty rating: Easy, mostly flat, a few hills, paved.

Distance: 2.25 miles.

Estimated time: 1.25 hours.

Services: Restrooms and water at the Sertoma Arts Center when open; a concession stand on the lake between the Sertoma Arts Center and the dam and spillway; emergency phone boxes on the trail.

Shelley Lake Trail

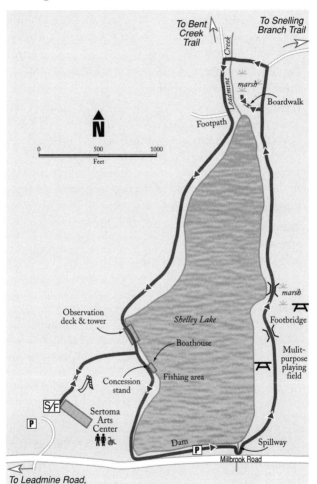

To Bent Creek Trail

To Snelling Branch Trail

Leadmine Creek

marsh

Boardwalk

Footpath

N

0   500   1000
Feet

Observation deck & tower

Shelley Lake

marsh

Footbridge

Boathouse

Multi-purpose playing field

Concession stand

Fishing area

S/F

P

Sertoma Arts Center

Dam

P

Spillway

Millbrook Road

To Leadmine Road, 440

Restrictions: Restrooms are available only when the Sertoma Arts Center is open. Bring water on the walk. Pets must be leashed and droppings picked up. Because of the isolated areas on parts of this walk, it is suggested that you walk with a partner.

For more information: Contact the City of Raleigh Department of Parks and Recreation.

Getting started: From I–440, take exit 7B, Glenwood Avenue, north, which is also US 70. Turn right onto Leadmine Road, the first right past the exit. Go 1 mile and turn right onto Millbrook Road. Look for the signs for the Sertoma Arts Center on the left less than 0.5 mile ahead. Park in the parking lot in front of the Sertoma Arts Center.

Public transportation: None.

Overview: The Shelley Lake Trail is a part of the Leadmine Creek Greenway in the Capital Area Greenway system and connects with several other spurs in the Leadmine Creek system: Snelling Branch, Bent Creek, Ironwood.

The walk around Shelley Lake is a popular trail in the greenway system. You will see boaters, hikers, bikers, and picnickers, as well as people fishing, sunning, and strolling. So pack a picnic, grab your camera, and join them in enjoying the walk around Shelley Lake.

The Walk

➤Facing the Sertoma Arts Center's main entrance, walk to the left of the building on the path leading down the hill toward a playground.

The greenway is marked with the Capital Area Greenway sign; look for it to the left and before you reach the playground. From here the paved trail descends a long hill under a canopy of birch trees.

At the foot of the hill you will see the lake and the boathouse. The observation deck and tower to the left are your return point after your loop around the lake. Paddleboats and johnboats are available for rent at the boathouse; the concession stand is here also.

➤Turn right to begin the loop around the lake. Millbrook Road parallels this portion of the walk.

You will walk past another parking area for the greenway on Millbrook Road. Benches on the right at the 0.25 milepost provide a place to sit and enjoy a panoramic view of Shelley Lake. As you walk, take advantage of the fitness trail markers located along this portion of the greenway providing easy-to-follow stretching activities.

➤At the end of the dam, curve right and follow the pavement. The multipurpose field here is popular for soccer, picnicking, kite flying, and sunbathing.

➤Descend the hill, turn left, and parallel the multipurpose field; Shelley Lake is ahead and to the left.

➤Cross the footbridge at the 0.5-mile point. Look for the picnic areas along this side of the lake.

➤At the next footbridge, you will be walking across a marsh, a good location for nature study. Stop at one of the many benches along the bridge and observe the wildlife. Although this is a heavily used trail, you may still spy birds, squirrels, an occasional deer, and other wildlife.

At the 1-mile point, the boardwalk on your left extends over the marsh, providing good opportunities to observe the marsh. A short loop trail takes you out to the boardwalk. Return to this point.

➤Turn left at the intersection, going downhill, where you will cross a footbridge over Leadmine Creek.

➤Turn left after you cross this footbridge. You will see other paved trails along this portion of the walk; these are connectors to the greenway leading to residential areas. The plan for the Capital Area Greenway is to form a single-trails network. These connectors are part of that process.

You are now following the western edge of the lake, paralleling Leadmine Creek and winding through a pine forest. The trail is wide and flat under the pines.

➤Continue straight at the next intersection where you can see the lake through the trees to your left. Just past the 1.75-mile point, the trail widens to accommodate an observation deck. Look out over the lake you have just circled and enjoy the view.

➤Cross the footbridge and walk up the hill. You have now completed the loop around the lake.

➤Turn right. Ascend the hill; you are back to the parking lot where you began the walk.

Walk 10
Blue Jay Point
Nature Walk

General location: Blue Jay Point County Park is located about 5 miles north of the Raleigh city limits on 236 acres adjacent to Falls Lake.

Special attractions: Fishing, walking, hiking, picnicking, a playground, and open-play fields are some of the amenities that await your visit to Blue Jay Point. However, the park's main attraction is its environmental education programming featured throughout the park but particularly at the Blue Jay Center for Environmental Education.

Difficulty rating: Easy, slight rolling hills as well as flat surfaces. All of the walk is paved except for the portion to Blue Jay Point, which is a walk through a forest on a dirt trail.

Blue Jay Point Nature Walk

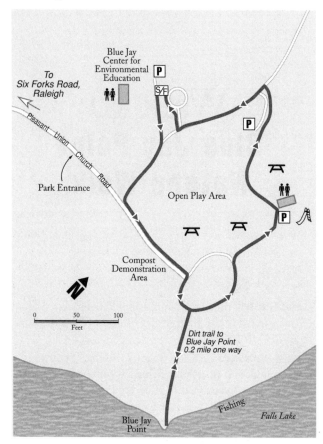

Walk 10

Distance: 0.75 mile.

Estimated time: 30 minutes.

Services: Restrooms and water fountains at the Center for Environmental Education and at the comfort station, which you will pass after you walk to Blue Jay Point. Bring water with you for the walk.

Restrictions: Pets must be kept on a 6-foot leash. Open fires are not allowed. Park only in designated places; the park speed limit is twenty miles per hour. Alcoholic beverages, firearms, hunting, camping, swimming, collection or removal of any plant or animal material, and amplified music are all prohibited. The park is closed Thanksgiving, Christmas Eve, Christmas Day, and New Year's Day.

For more information: Contact Blue Jay Point County Park.

Getting started: Take exit 8, Six Forks Road, off I–440 and go north. After traveling about 5 miles, you will be at the edge of the Raleigh city limits. You are approximately 5 miles from the park now. Stay on Six Forks Road. Just past the Bayleaf Fire Station, the road makes a sharp turn to the left. Follow Six Forks Road and turn left here rather than going straight. You will begin to see part of the Falls Lake Reservoir. Look for signs for Blue Jay Point County Park. Turn left onto Pleasant Union Church Road, which ends on the park's premises. Drive to the first intersection inside the park, and turn left.

Just past the Blue Jay Center for Environmental Education on your left, turn left into the visitor parking lot, which is the starting point for this walk.

Public transportation: None.

Overview: The focal point of this park is environmental education. When you add the natural beauty of Blue Jay Point County Park with its hardwood and pine forests, gently rolling hills, and large grassy fields, you have an ideal walk for environmentalists as well as parents and children. School groups regularly visit the park, especially the center for environmental education.

If you visit in spring, summer, or fall, be sure to visit the garden located to the left of the center for environmental education. An active garden, it is designed to demonstrate what people can do in their backyards to develop wildlife habitats.

Spend some time in the natural wood and brick center for environmental education, whose purpose is to educate people about the environment. Open and airy, it contains classrooms, meeting rooms, and environmental displays.

A large floor-to-ceiling display designed to teach children how we get water into our homes shows the process for attaining water from the time it leaves the lake to the point where the faucet is turned on in a kitchen. Other displays depict the growth of a community, the effects of humans on the environment, and water pollution and conservation, all designed for children to comprehend. As adults you will more than likely enjoy them also. You can pick up some of the many environmental education brochures the center offers. Other activities for children in the center make it a pleasant place to spend an hour or so, either before or after your walk.

Wooded picnic areas are popular spots at Blue Jay Point County Park.

The Walk

➤From the stop sign at the circular drive in the parking area, turn right.

➤Turn left at the next stop sign. A compost demonstration area on your right down this street shows how compost is produced. Steps on your left lead up to an open playing field and a picnic area.

➤Walk right around the traffic circle. In the traffic circle, look for a sign for the Blue Jay Point trail, a 0.2 mile trail that leads to Blue Jay Point.

➤Follow this sign and go to your right, walking on the dirt trail. Shortly you will enter a hardwood and pine forest. This trail is marked with blue blazes painted on signs and on tree trunks, so follow the blazes and you will not get lost on this well-marked trail.

This is an easy, slightly downhill walk. Watch for tree roots, some of which have grown out into the trail and could cause you to stumble. Look up at the canopy of maples, oaks, and pines and other evergreens. Although this is a popular walk and you may meet other walkers, you will also have a feeling of remoteness, both in the woods and once you reach Blue Jay Point.

When you reach the point, stop and rest, enjoying the expansive lake view. You are standing on a sandy point looking out onto Lower Barton Creek, a portion of Falls Lake. Look down and to your left and you might see beavers and the results of their work.

After you have rested and enjoyed the view, retrace your steps to the traffic circle. You will be walking steadily up a slight hill on the way back, so take your time, rest frequently, take sips of water, and enjoy your surroundings.

Walk 10

➤In the traffic circle, turn right. You will see a playground and a comfort station with water fountains near the next parking area. If you are walking with children, they will enjoy the chance to play at the playground for a few minutes before you continue your walk. Benches provide a place to rest while they play.

➤Stand facing the comfort station and look for the paved trail to the left. Take this trail.

You will see a wooded picnic area on your right and the open playing field on your left as you walk this portion of the trail. Good vistas of the park are available to your left as you walk.

➤At the next parking lot, turn left.

➤Turn right at the next paved street and you are back at your starting point.

Of Interest

Other Trails in Blue Jay Point County Park

Want more exercise? Other walking trails as well as hiking trails in the park provide a total of 4 miles of trails within the park's boundaries. At the Center pick up a brochure describing these walking and hiking trails. Some of the walks similar to the walk to Blue Jay Point that you might enjoy are listed and briefly described here.

Sandy Point Trail: Look for signs leading to the Lodge. From the lodge, this trail is a 0.2-mile walk to Sandy Point, which is north of and similar to Blue Jay Point.

Laurel Loop Trail: This 0.2-mile loop goes from the park's playground to the shore of Falls Lake. The north-facing slope provides an excellent environment for the hardy mountain laurel, which you will see on this walk.

Walk 11
City Sights

General location: Explore the heart of downtown Durham in a walk through the historic areas of the business district.

Special attractions: Historic landmarks, varied architecture, Durham Convention and Visitors Bureau, Carolina Theatre, urban parks, art galleries, outdoor murals.

Difficulty rating: Easy, mostly flat, sidewalks; some slight, short inclines.

Distance: 0.8 mile.

Estimated time: 30 minutes.

Services: Several restaurants and restrooms. Wheelchair-accessible restrooms at the Marriott Hotel, Carolina Theatre, and Durham Convention and Visitors Bureau.

Restrictions: Dogs must be leashed and droppings picked up. Wheelchair-accessible bathrooms are available at the

City Sights

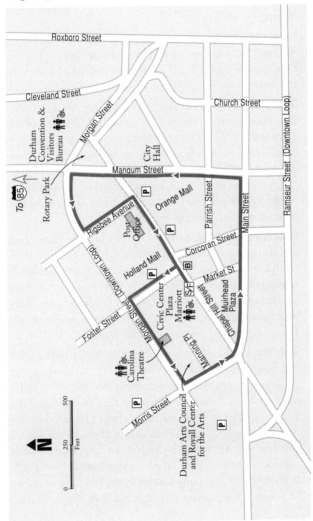

Marriott Hotel anytime and at the Carolina Theatre and the convention and visitors bureau only during business hours.

For more information: Contact the Durham Convention and Visitors Bureau for information about city sights and events and the Carolina Theatre and the Royall Center for the Arts for events and prices.

Getting started: This walk begins at the Durham Marriott at 201 Foster Street. From I–85, take the Durham downtown exit 177A. Turn right onto Morgan Street (also called the Downtown Loop). Turn left onto Foster Street; the Marriott Hotel and Civic Center complex are on the right. Park in the city lot across from the Marriott Hotel, in the People's Security Insurance Building parking deck or at meters on Morgan Street.

Public transportation: Most buses in the Durham Area Transit Authority (DATA) go within a few blocks of or directly to downtown: buses 2, 3, 4, 5, 7, 8, 9, 12 run Monday through Saturday, generally from 5:30 A.M. to 11:30 P.M. Contact DATA for times, fares, and accessibility. These buses stop near the Marriott Hotel at the intersection of Foster, Corcoran, and Chapel Hill Streets.

Overview: Durham, a city set in the center of a state in the hot South, is surprisingly cool looking, even when temperatures climb. Abundant trees in downtown—particularly on Main Street—and small urban parks, many with the cool sound of water fountains, help Durham feel cool; its nickname is City of Trees. When the trees leaf out, you feel like you are walking through an urban forest of tall buildings fronted with crepe myrtles, maples, and oaks. Spring brings flowering forsythia, azaleas, and dogwoods to enhance the greening of downtown. In the winter, bare trees allow the walker an even better view of the buildings. Even a January walk can be pleasant in this Southern city.

As you walk, notice some of the historic buildings. Many of the older ones were once scheduled to be removed and replaced by modern structures. Some newer buildings have indeed replaced more historic ones, making downtown a varied blend of old and new. Downtown Durham was North Carolina's first commercial district to be added to the National Register of Historic Places due to Durham's preservation efforts. The city's pride in its history and its future is nowhere more evident than downtown.

An assortment of places to explore on this walk include small parks with benches, seasonal flowers and fountains, and historic buildings with interesting, varied architecture and historical significance. Try some of the restaurants. Dine in or pick up coffee and a bagel or sandwich to take with you to one of the park benches or picnic tables. Sunny, warm January days often find people sitting on park benches, sipping coffee and chatting.

Be sure to see the outdoor murals and visit art galleries and art centers along this walk. The city takes pride in the art it has brought downtown.

The Walk

Note: The Durham Convention and Visitors Bureau has a walking tour of downtown Durham and has collected information about buildings on this walk, some of which appears here.

►At the Chapel Hill Street entrance to the Marriott Hotel, turn left onto Chapel Hill Street and walk to the intersection of Foster and Chapel Hill Streets.

➤Turn left onto Foster Street. The hotel is on your left. As you pass the fountains, you will see the Civic Center Plaza.

The terra-cotta roof of the Durham Armory, the original Durham Civic Center, is on your right. Fountains at the Civic Center Plaza make an inviting place to enjoy the sights and sounds of the flowing water, which muffles the street noise.

➤Turn left onto Morgan Street and walk toward the fountains. The building across the street is the Downtown YMCA Family Center.

As you walk along Morgan Street, look upward at the green foliage spilling over the sides of the multileveled, terraced parking deck of the fourteen-story People's Security Insurance Building. To your left is the Carolina Theatre.

Just past the Carolina Theatre, you will continue to hear the fountains and falling water. The fountains, part of the People's Security Insurance complex, lend a feeling of serenity. Wheelchair users will encounter a slight incline along this portion of Morgan Street.

➤When you reach Morris Street, turn left. The Durham Arts Council and the Royall Center for the Arts are on the corner. Royall Center houses eighteen arts organizations. Call for information about classes and performances. Benches in front of the arts council building and an interesting granite statuary collection provide unusual seating at the corner of Morris Street and Manning Place. Emily Weinstein's mural on the wall of the Penny Furniture Building depicts the Eno River just outside Durham. Morris ends at Chapel Hill Street.

➤Turn left onto Main Street. Along this street, you will find several benches where you can stop, rest, and enjoy downtown sights.

Walk 11

The Carolina Theatre

This 1926 beaux arts historic landmark arts complex was renovated in 1992. When movies were added in the 1930s, it became the Carolina Theatre. Fletcher Hall, a 1,014-seat auditorium is used for performing arts, sales meetings, conferences, and lectures. Call for information about movies, performances, and other events.

To explore this building, walk left past the fountains and up the exterior steps to the cinema lobby or through the video rental store at street level, where there are elevators. Wheelchair-accessible bathrooms are on both levels. Note the arched 18-foot windows. The cinemas feature award-winning foreign and independent films and stadium-style seating.

Kirby lobby through the door adjacent to the video rental store is the entrance to Fletcher Hall and Connie Moses Ballroom. Reproductions of antique light fixtures and a green marble-top bar adorn Kirby lobby. Connie Moses Ballroom contains replicas of the original crystal chandeliers on its 24-foot cathedral ceiling.

You are at Five Points/Muirhead Plaza, which is a small brick-paved park with picnic tables, trees, and seasonal flowers. BC Headache Powder was invented on this site in 1910. Each September 60,000 festival-goers crowd this park and downtown for CenterFest, the state's oldest and largest street fair.

If bookstores attract you, turn right onto Chapel Hill Street at Muirhead Plaza and walk one-half block to the Book Exchange, billed as the South's greatest used book store. Return to Main Street at Muirhead Plaza and resume your walk.

Note the red-tiled roof of Triangle Bank, a triangular-shaped building beside Muirhead Plaza. Also observe the interesting architecture on your left, some of which is briefly noted here.

Number 331: The 1933 Snow Building features classic art deco design.

Number 309: The building's distinguishing feature, the letter *H*, is enscrolled several times near the top of the building. This 1925 Georgian revival–style building is known today as the Old Hill Building, commissioned by John Sprunt Hill—the *H* is his monogram.

Number 302: The 1909 Spanish mission–style Temple Building is now home to a bank. The six-story Trust

Durham's skyline. (Courtesy Durham Convention and Visitors Bureau)

Building on your left at the corner of Main and Market Streets, built in 1905 in the Renaissance revival style, was at one time the tallest building in the state. Notice its distinctive rounded corners.

Number 111 Corcoran Street: The Hill Building, now the Central Carolina Bank, was designed by the architects of the Empire State Building. Resemblances to the New York landmark include the stepped-back design. Its seventeen stories completed in 1937 replaced Durham's Trust Building as North Carolina's tallest.

Number 124: The old Woolworth Building is the site of a 1960s civil rights sit-in. The wall mural, *Jazzy Downtown,* is by Michael Brown.

Of Interest

The Woolworth's Sit-ins

The first sit-in occurred in Durham in 1957. The Reverend Douglas E. Moore of Asbury Temple took students from North Carolina College for Negroes—later North Carolina Central University—to the white section of the Royal Ice Cream Company Store on Roxboro Street. They asked for service but were arrested for trespassing after they sat down.

Local college and high school students trained by Reverend Moore visited this Woolworth's on February 8, 1960. Store personnel refused to serve them and closed the lunch counter. This sit-in was the first that Dr. Martin Luther King Jr. attended. Sit-ins also were organized at Kress's lunch counter; at Rose's department store, management even removed the counter stools to avoid serving blacks. However, the NAACP and others supported the students' efforts, and by the end of 1960 Durham's lunch counters were integrated, thanks to these brave students.

In the late 1840s, the lot opposite the Woolworth Building was the site of Pandora's Box, the home of Dr. Bartlett Durham, for whom Durham is named. The next building on this lot, the Hotel Clairborne—later the Carolina Hotel—burned in 1907. The next occupant was the First National Bank; the lot is now home to Nation's Bank.

Number 117: Be sure to look at the ornate work on the second story of this 1927 neoclassical revival–style building.

Number 111: The 1893 Romanesque revival Coulter Building is the oldest building inside the Downtown Loop.

Number 101: The 1932 art deco Kress Building (K-Mart) is now the Durham office of the Raleigh *News and Observer*. Note the rounded glass display windows; the ornate, colorful carvings; and the word *Kress* at the top center of the building.

►Turn left onto Mangum Street. The small park 1 block ahead on your left is a narrow, brick tree-lined walkway known as Orange Mall. Orange of Durham, a brand of tobacco popular in the nineteenth century, gave this pedestrian mall its name.

At the intersection of City Hall Plaza and Mangum Street, you are in front of Durham City Hall. Look to the right at this intersection for a view of the Ionic columns and portico of the 1927 neoclassical revival First Baptist Church at 414 Cleveland Street.

One block past city hall, Rotary Park contains intriguing rockwork, perennial and annual flowers, and a fountain. One entrance to this round park has steps; two entrances are accessible to wheelchairs.

Durham Convention and Visitors Bureau at 101 Morgan Street offers brochures, schedules, and information as well as kiosks that picture Durham's attractions, and wheelchair-accessible bathrooms during business hours. A knowledgeable, friendly, helpful staff is eager to help you enjoy your stay in Durham.

➤At the intersection of Mangum and Morgan Streets, turn left onto Morgan Street. In the skyline directly ahead is the People's Security Insurance Building.

➤Turn left onto Rigsbee Avenue. Wheelchair users, note a slight incline of a short distance in this portion of Rigsbee Avenue.

➤Turn right onto Chapel Hill Street where Rigsbee Avenue dead-ends. The post office at 323 Chapel Hill Street, a 1934 neoclassical revival–style building, stands where Union general William Sherman camped with his troops. Three miles from here, at a farm known as Bennett Place, he negotiated the largest surrender of the Civil War. Note the beautiful lamps and large Doric columns of the front facade. An oversized, ornately designed flagpole stands in front.

Notice also the colorful metal sculptures in the front of the Artomatic Gallery on your right. This artist-run gallery exhibits works by local artists. Upstairs, Durham Artsplace provides studios for artists. Stop and browse if you have time. The adjoining Amoore Art Studio features pencil drawings of 1930s through 1950s downtown Durham by Aaron Michael Moore, III.

➤At the intersection of Chapel Hill and Foster Streets, you will be back at the Marriott Hotel and the starting point of the walk.

Walk 12
Campus and Shopping

General location: Brightleaf Square, a tobacco warehouse converted into a shopping center, and historic 9th Street shopping district are the anchors for this walk through Duke University's East Campus and an old neighborhood bordering the university.

Special attractions: Brightleaf Square, Historic 9th Street, Duke University East Campus, Duke University Museum of Art.

Difficulty rating: Easy, mostly flat, sidewalks, some moderate, short inclines.

Distance: 2.8 miles.

Estimated time: 2.5 hours.

Walk 12

Services: Parking, restaurants, restrooms.

Restrictions: Dogs must be leashed and their droppings picked up.

For more information: Contact the Durham Convention and Visitors Bureau, Brightleaf Square, or Duke University Museum of Art.

Getting started: This walk begins at Brightleaf Square. From I–85, take Durham downtown exit 177A. Turn right onto Morgan Street and then right onto Main Street. Brightleaf Square is two blocks ahead on the left at Gregson and Main Streets. Parking lots are on Main Street near Brightleaf Square.

Public transportation: Buses 1, 10, and 11 serve Brightleaf Square Monday through Saturday, in general from about 5:30 A.M. to 11:30 P.M. Contact Durham Area Transit Authority (DATA) for times, fares, and accessibility.

Overview: If you enjoy city traffic, college campuses, museums, eclectic shops, and restaurants, this walk is for you. Busy sidewalks take you past two unique shopping areas: Brightleaf Square and historic 9th Street. You will border the East Campus of Duke University for much of your walk. The campus, with its beautiful expansive grounds, offers a refreshing contrast to the bustle and traffic.

Main Street parallels the railroad, which transports tobacco to and from the massive brick tobacco warehouses downtown. In *A History of Durham County, North Carolina,* Jean Anderson describes how Durham's tobacco warehouses solved the problem farmers had of displaying their tobacco to potential buyers. Before 1871, North Carolina tobacco farmers hauled their tobacco from factory to factory looking for a buyer, or they shipped it to Virginia warehouses at great expense. Recognizing the problem,

Campus and Shopping

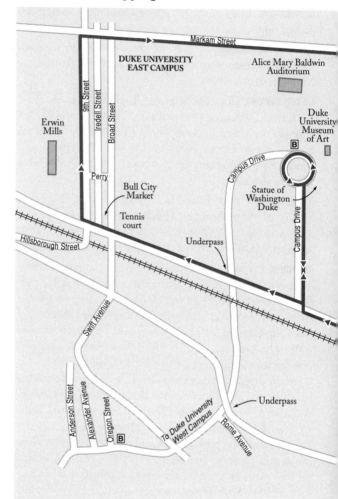

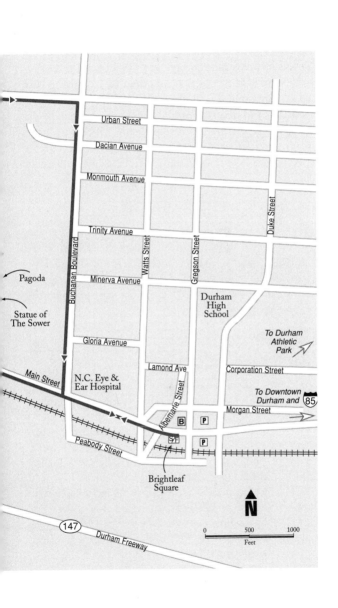

William T. Blackwell built the first tobacco warehouse in Durham in 1871 at the corner of today's Pettigrew and Blackwell Streets. In the first year, 700,000 pounds of tobacco were sold in this warehouse; in the following year, two million pounds were sold.

Much of Durham's history is linked to tobacco. Just as strong are Durham's links to medicine. Durham became the City of Medicine in 1981 and shifted from a tobacco-based economy to one based on medicine and health care.

The Walk

Note: Before you begin your walk, you may want to explore some of the stores in Brightleaf Square. Brightleaf Square contains a variety of shops, including book shops, music shops, and galleries, as well as restaurants. If you decide to shop here, be sure to walk behind the portion that faces

Of Interest

Why Is It Called Brightleaf?

Brightleaf is the name of a type of tobacco plant. After the Civil War, local farmers were looking for a cash crop that would be in high demand, provide them with needed revenues, and not be overly labor intensive. Because the soldiers on both sides of the Civil War loved and wanted more of the locally grown tobacco, the farmers around Durham turned to tobacco for a living.

The local land was right for a new leaf of tobacco that grew well in the area's light, sandy soil. The plant produced a leaf lighter in color than that produced in the eastern part of the state. Hence, the Bright Tobacco Belt, which later became Brightleaf.

Campus Drive on Duke University's East Campus attracts joggers and walkers.

Main Street and see the beautiful courtyard and the other shops in the Brightleaf shopping district.

➤Start at the Main Street entrance to Brightleaf Square.

On the Brightleaf Square building at the corner of Gregson and Main Street is a plaque that reads, LIGGETT AND MYERS TOBACCO COMPANY, YUILLE WAREHOUSE, 1904. This is one of downtown's many beautiful brick turn-of-the-century tobacco warehouses. Some have been converted to condos, office space, or—in the case of Brightleaf Square—a beautiful shopping area. The Yuille warehouse, named for Thomas D. Yuille, an American Tobacco Company executive, was converted into this popular shopping complex and renamed Brightleaf Square.

➤Leaving Brightleaf Square, turn left onto Main Street away from the downtown area. You will pass small, interesting restaurants on your right as you walk up a slight incline, with funeral homes and other businesses on your left.

On your right is N. C. Eye & Ear Hospital. Number 1113, the Hall-Wynn Funeral Service and Cremation, was the site of the viewing of the exhumed body of Dr. B. L. Durham, Durham's namesake.

➤After crossing Buchanan Boulevard, you will approach the main entrance to East Campus of Duke University and follow the stone wall that borders the campus, originally known as Trinity College.

➤At the next traffic light, turn right at the stone columns onto Campus Drive. Along this portion of the campus you will see the statue of *The Sower* in front of a pagoda.

➤Continue along the sidewalk paralleling Campus Drive until you reach the traffic circle. A statue of Washington Duke, created by Edward Valentine and unveiled in 1980,

Dr. Bartlett Leonidus Durham (1824–59)

Durham County was named for Dr. Bartlett Leonidus Durham, the owner of the land on which the railroad station, which was the nucleus of what was to become the city of Durham, was located. Despite the *Dr.* in front of his name, no record exists of Durham attending medical school. His family claimed he took a course in medicine in Philadelphia in November 1845.

Neighbors remembered this colorful character as a friendly, hard-drinking, and fun-loving man. He would often rally friends to serenade local townswomen with horns, fiddles, and banjos. Durham reputedly loved to chase women, which got him into some trouble—after his death.

One of these women, Susan Ann Clements, waited until after Dr. Durham's death on February 2, 1859, to accuse him of fathering her son Romulus. The case was heard by three lower courts before the North Carolina Supreme Court ruled against her, making it impossible for her to receive financial support from Durham's estate.

Another curious event in Dr. Durham's colorful life occurred after his death. He was buried in the Snipes family graveyard. But Durham's American Business Club concluded that Durham had been inadequately honored at the time of his death. So in 1933, seventy-four years after he died, his body was exhumed and exhibited at the Hall-Wynne funeral parlor. It was tactfully noted at the time of the exhibition that his body was well preserved. Six months later he was reburied in Maplewood Cemetery at Moorehead Avenue and Chapel Hill Street in a grave marked by a granite tombstone on which his middle name, birth date, and death date are incorrect. Let us hope his body is allowed to rest in peace and no other after-death experiences affect his repose.

Of Interest

From Trinity College to Duke University

Duke began life as Union Institute in 1838 in Randolph County, about 75 miles northwest of its present site. Established by Methodists and Quakers in a one-room log building, Union became Normal College and later Trinity College. In May 1889, Pres. John Franklin Crowell wanted to improve the college's status and growth, so he announced that the school was available to be moved to another location.

Raleigh citizens offered a sum of money to have the college moved there, but Washington Duke countered with an offer of $85,000, and Julian S. Carr donated sixty-two acres in Durham's Blackwell Park. In September 1892, Trinity College, with its possessions loaded into one boxcar, arrived in Durham and became the city's first institute of higher learning.

By 1895 Trinity College had twelve professors and was growing. In 1924 the status of the college improved considerably when James B. Duke announced a major gift to Trinity on the condition that the name of the college be changed to Duke. The trustees accepted his offer, and the school's name was changed.

sits here. Duke was a generous donor to Trinity College, and after his death friends commissioned the statue to honor him.

The statue portrays Washington Duke sitting in a large leather-looking armchair, legs crossed, looking straight ahead. He appears to be pondering serious topics while examining visitors to his campus.

The colorful banners of Duke University Museum of Art (DUMA) are on the brick building to the right on the

Walk 12

Duke Landmarks: *The Sower*

James B. Duke purchased *The Sower* in Europe and placed the sculpture on his New Jersey estate. John C. Kilgo, a former president of Trinity, admired the statue while visiting Duke's estate, so Duke donated it to the college.

The statue depicts a seventeenth-century peasant sowing his fields. The seeds he is sowing are in a bag over his shoulder; his hand is outstretched to broadcast seed onto the ground.

In the 1930s, campus women's privileges were severely restricted; however, female students were permitted to walk on this part of the campus and could walk freely by the statue. Couples placed pennies in the sower's outstretched hand, and could claim a kiss from their partner if the pennies were gone when they returned. Today one can still occasionally find pennies in the outstretched hand of *The Sower*, although some modern-day parents of Duke students claim that the statue represents Duke sons and daughters with hands extended to receive more money for campus life.

main quad of East Campus; if time permits, visit the museum. Tours are available; contact the museum for information.

At this point you may want to walk deeper into the quad to get a better view of Baldwin Auditorium. If you do, return to this point to continue your walk.

The Alice Mary Baldwin Auditorium in the center of the quad is modeled after the Thomas Jefferson Library, University of Virginia. Baldwin, with its Ionic portico and circular dome auditorium in the neoclassical revival style, is the focus of the East Campus quadrangle. Alice Mary Baldwin was dean of the Women's College from 1926 to 1947 and the first woman at Duke to obtain full faculty status; much of her tenure was spent advocating equality for women on campus.

The traffic circle is the site of a much-used bus stop for students traveling the 2 miles from the East to the West Campus.

➤Return to Main Street by walking under the canopy of mature oak trees along Campus Drive.

The ROTC and Kenan Ethics programs are among those housed in the putty-colored building to your right.

➤At the intersection of Campus and Main Streets, turn right at the stone columns and continue along Main

Of Interest

The Duke Blue Devils

Duke's mascot, the Blue Devil, is named for a troop of World War I French soldiers, famous for their dark blue uniforms, berets, and capes. To raise money for the war effort, the French Blue Devils toured the United States when this country entered the war.

Popular in America, they were immortalized in the Irving Berlin song, "The Blue Devils of France," with its lyrics, "strong and active, most attractive . . . these Devils, the Blue Devils of France."

When postwar Trinity College began playing football in 1927 after a twenty-five-year ban due to the war, the student newspaper, the *Chronicle,* began a search for a team name. Since the school colors were dark blue and white and the French Blue Devils were so popular, the name quickly caught on.

Street, which is bordered on the left by the railroad tracks and on the right by East Campus.

After you walk approximately 0.2 mile, you will cross over Campus Drive, which connects East and West Campuses. As you cross, look down at the graffiti on the walls of the overpass, much of which is Duke blue for the Duke Blue Devils.

➤Continue along Main Street, where you will walk by more Duke buildings on the right, many shadowed by magnolia trees. In May and June you will enjoy the sweet fragrance of magnolia blossoms.

As you cross Swift Avenue, which is Broad Street to the right, you will have reached the end of the walled area of Duke University. You will pick up the walk beside the wall in back of the campus later in this walk. Duke's tennis courts are on your right.

Bull City Market, the shopping center on the right, has several places to stop for refreshments: Broad Street Diner, Ben & Jerry's ice cream, PieWorks, and others. Feeling adventurous? Stop at Wellspring Grocery and create a picnic lunch to enjoy on the university grounds. Wellspring also provides outdoor dining—a good place to drink an espresso and people watch. Return to Main Street in front of Bull City Market.

To your right at the junction of Iredell and Main Streets, you will notice the bright red doors of St. Joseph's Episcopal Church.

➤At the junction of Main and 9th Streets, turn right onto 9th Street. This is a popular Durham shopping district, which grew up seventy-five years ago alongside Erwin Cotton Mills.

As you walk along, look left at Erwin Cotton Mills, the large brick structure 1 block away. Now home to offices and apartments, it was once the world's largest manufacturer of denim.

A variety of small shops, including bookstores, coffee shops, music shops, art studios, an organic grocery, and more await you on 9th Street.

➤Turn right onto Markham Street.

You are leaving the 9th Street shopping district and coming back to the area where East Campus will be on your right; a residential area is on your left. Along Markham Street, you will find a few small restaurants and the bookstore, Books Do Furnish a Room.

As you cross Broad Street, you will once again be walking along the rock wall that surrounds East Campus. The Branson Theater is on your right. Just up the street is an ivy-covered wall, which is the back of the Mary Duke Biddle Music Building.

➤At the intersection of Markham and Buchanan Streets, turn right onto Buchanan Street.

At 402 Buchanan Street, the Ryan Research Center Institute of Parapsychology—a world-famous center for the study of ESP and other unusual mental phenomena—offers a library, a bookstore, and exhibits. Tours of labs featuring historical photographs, work areas, and a history of the center are scheduled twice monthly; a public meeting is held every Thursday at noon. Contact the center for further information.

➤At the top of the slight incline on Buchanan Street, turn left onto Main Street. The N. C. Eye and Ear Hospital is now on your left.

At the intersection of Main, Morgan, and Watts Streets, look ahead for a view of the Durham skyline. You will see the prominent Liggett Group, Inc. billboard directly over Brightleaf Square and the North Carolina Mutual Life Insurance just to its right. Notice the airwalks connecting the warehouses of The Liggett Group, formerly the Liggett and Myers Tobacco Company, which relocated to Mebane, North Carolina.

Continue along Main Street until you reach the main entrance of Brightleaf Square, your starting point.

Walk 13
Bull Durham

General location: Explore the world of Bull Durham baseball in this walk that takes you from the old Durham Athletic Park through part of downtown to the new Durham Bulls Athletic Park.

Special attractions: Durham Athletic Park, Durham Bulls Athletic Park, downtown Durham.

Difficulty rating: Easy, mostly flat, paved sidewalk.

Distance: 2 miles.

Estimated time: 1 hour.

Services: Parking, restaurants, restrooms.

Restrictions: Dogs must be leashed and droppings picked up. Admission charge for baseball games.

For more information: Contact the Durham Convention and Visitors Bureau. Contact the Durham Athletic Park for

Bull Durham

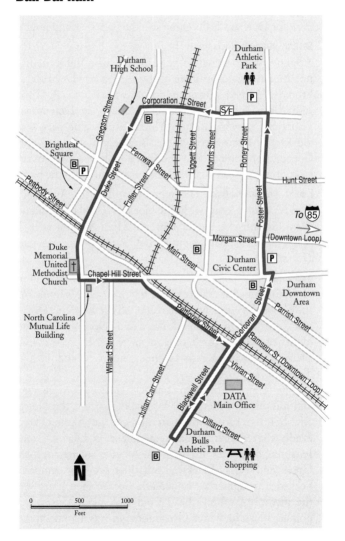

Durham Braves ticket and schedule information, including prices and hours. Contact the Durham Bulls Athletic Park for Durham Bulls game schedules, prices, and hours.

Getting started: This walk begins at the historic Durham Athletic Park, original home of the Durham Bulls, the International League affiliate of the Tampa Bay Devil Rays. From I–85, take Durham downtown exit 177A. Turn right onto Morgan Street, also called the Downtown Loop, and then right onto Morris Street. The park is 2 blocks up Morris Street at the intersection of Morris and Corporation Streets. You will find a gravel parking lot on Corporation Street in front of the main gate into the park.

Public transportation: Durham Area Transit Authority (DATA) bus 1 goes within 1 block of Durham Athletic Park. Get off the bus at Durham High School; walk 1 block east to the park. Contact DATA for times, fares, and accessibility.

Overview: Durham Athletic Park was the home of the Durham Bulls baseball team for fifty years and is home for the Durham Braves baseball team and the Durham Dragons softball team. The park has had a colorful past, some of which was captured on film in the 1987 movie *Bull Durham,* starring Kevin Costner, Susan Sarandon, and Tim Robbins.

The origin of the team's bull logo goes back to the cigarette industry. After Civil War soldiers from the North and South returned to their homes, they remembered fondly the excellent tobacco produced in Durham, and sent mail orders for the product. As sales increased, John Green and W. T. Blackwell felt their growing company needed a recognizable trademark. So the men borrowed the picture of a bull's head from Coleman's Mustard, a popular mustard, which Green thought was manufactured in Durham, England. With a bull as its picture and a tobacco product manufactured in Durham, the cigarettes soon became known as *Bull Durham.*

Julian S. Carr ran an extensive advertising campaign in the 1870s and 1880s to popularize the logo. The sign appeared everywhere—on barns and billboards throughout the United States, in Europe, and in the Orient. A Bull Durham sign was actually found on one of the Egyptian pyramids. The slogan accompanying the logo was "Durham Renowned the World Round," and so it was. The sign was also on billboards in most American ballparks. The company stepped up the advertising by offering $50 to any player who hit the bull with a batted ball.

You can still see the bull on signs at both the historic park and the new Durham Bulls Athletic Park. Buy a ticket and visit the well-appointed new ballpark. If you are lucky, you will see a Durham Bulls home run and the billboard bull wag his tail, flicker his red eyes, and snort lustily his support of his home team.

The Walk

➤Begin your walk at Durham Athletic Park in front of the blue turret with the Durham Bulls logo of a large orange *D* on a blue background and a bull jumping through the *D.*

The Durham Bulls, founded in 1902, made this park home from 1926 to 1994. The park is now the home of the Durham Braves, a summer team made up of star college baseball players who play for free to maintain NCAA eligibility. The Durham Dragons, one of six women's fastpitch softball teams across the nation, also play in this park.

Durham Bulls Athletic Park in downtown Durham. (Courtesy Durham Convention and Visitors Bureau)

Walk around the inside of the stadium; if a game is in progress, you may be charged admission. The movie *Bull Durham* was shot in this stadium, and during filming, star Susan Sarandon sat in box U.

➤Walk out of Durham Athletic Park and turn right onto Corporation Street. At the top of the slight incline, you will cross a set of railroad tracks. Many of the brick tobacco warehouses along this street have been converted into spaces for industries, law offices, and condos.

➤ Turn left onto Duke Street and walk under the canopy of mature oak trees. Across the street are more warehouses. As you approach the intersection of Duke and Morgan Streets, look left and notice the beautiful wrought-iron fencing on the warehouses, a distinctive trademark of these tobacco buildings.

After crossing Morgan Street, notice the Tobacco Roadhouse and Brew Pub on your right. After you cross the alley just beyond the brew pub, look up at the top of the next building on your right for an old Studebaker sign that marks this building as a former car dealership.

To your right when you cross Main Street is Brightleaf Square, a tobacco warehouse complex that has been turned into a series of architecturally distinctive shops and restaurants. On your left at this intersection, note the employee airwalks that connect the buildings of Liggett and Myers Tobacco Company.

Fowler's Gourmet Grocery on your right just before you cross Peabody Street is a good place to get a soft drink, a gourmet picnic, or lunch. You can see bread being made here and buy a cup of gourmet coffee. Dine at a table, or make up a picnic to take with you to the ballgame.

➤At the intersection of Peabody and Duke Streets, cross and continue on the sidewalk on the right side of Duke Street. You will then cross railroad tracks.

You will have a good view of the twin towers and stained-glass windows of Duke Memorial United Methodist Church, a 1907 Gothic revival–style church

John Merrick and Black Wall Street

North Carolina Mutual Life Insurance is one of the largest African-American owned and managed financial institutions in the world. Its success is due largely to the efforts of John Merrick and other black businesspeople, who in 1898 began to provide life insurance for African-Americans.

Merrick was the son of an ex-slave and a white man. As a young man he was a bootblack in a Raleigh barber shop. John Wright worked in the same barber shop and was impressed by the young, hardworking Merrick. In 1880 he persuaded Merrick to move to Durham with him and to work in his barber shop. Merrick eventually bought Wright's business and opened more shops.

Merrick was now a prominent Durham businessman and member of the Royal Knights of King David, a semi-religious fraternal and beneficial society for health and life insurance. He knew two realities for African-Americans: They had short life expectancies because of poor health and poverty, and they found it difficult if not impossible to obtain insurance at white-owned insurance companies.

Merrick sought investors and soon opened North Carolina Mutual and Provident Society, later the North Carolina Mutual Life Insurance Company, on Parrish Street.

The insurance company had a rough start. Initially several investors pulled out, but soon it succeeded. The company bought additional property on Parrish Street, and by 1910 a commercial district flourished there with African-American–owned clothing stores, a drugstore, and newspaper offices. Parrish Street became known as Black Wall Street, and Durham earned the title City of the New South because of the success of its black businesspeople. The insurance company remained on Parrish until 1966, when it moved to its present site on Chapel Hill Street.

named for Washington Duke. The church has a Holtkamp organ and a ten-bell manual carillon; carillon performances are presented nightly. You may want to interrupt your walk to go inside the church, where you will find information and a printed guide to the stained-glass windows. Return to this spot to continue your walk.

➤At the intersection of Chapel Hill and Duke Streets, turn left onto Chapel Hill Street. On the right at number 411 is North Carolina Mutual Life Insurance.

As you walk down the slight incline, look left for another view of the Liggett and Myers Tobacco warehouse buildings and a view of the Durham skyline.

Halfway down this incline, just before you reach Pettigrew Street, you will walk past the Durham Amtrak railroad station on your left. Look back to your left at the *Locomotive* mural, on the side of the building. This painting by Michael Brown is an interesting, colorful close-up of the wheels of a locomotive.

➤Turn right onto Pettigrew Street just before you get to the railroad overpass. Continue on the sidewalk to the right that parallels the railroad tracks alongside the street. Durham Bulls banners decorate the streetlight posts here; to the left is the Durham skyline.

Just before you reach the intersection of Pettigrew and Julian Carr Streets, look to your right for the famous Lucky Strike logos on the old Lucky Strike water tower and the old smokestack. Now this area is surrounded by a new complex of residences, offices, and condos.

You are walking alongside the beautiful 1900 Blackwell Hill warehouse. Note the detailed variegated patterns of the bricks.

➤Turn right onto Blackwell Street. You will see the Durham Bulls Athletic Park and the silhouette of the bull who stands over the park and snorts and wags his tail when his team scores a run.

The main terminal of the Durham Area Transit Authority (DATA) is to your left at 111 Vivian Street. Across the street, note the Italianate 1874 Bull Durham Building. A national historic landmark, it was built when W. T. Blackwell and Company, developer of the world-renowned Bull Durham brand, was at the height of its success.

Stay on the sidewalk until you reach the main entrance to the Durham Bulls Athletic Park. The official Bull Durham memorabilia shop is on the left. Restrooms are available in the park; you will find a children's playground and a picnic area inside the park. You might want to purchase tickets for a game if it is baseball season and the Bulls are playing. After you explore the park, return to the main entrance.

➤As you leave the stadium entrance, turn right and walk back up Blackwell Street toward downtown Durham.

Blackwell becomes Corcoran Street after you cross Pettigrew. Continue along Corcoran Street.

Before you cross Parrish Street, look right at the Merchant's and Farmer's Bank, an ornate building at number 116. You will notice two interesting balconies on this 1921 neoclassical revival building. A National Historic Landmark, it was built on the site of North Carolina Mutual's first headquarters and serves as a reminder of the racial progress evidenced by the rise of this black-owned business.

➤Turn left onto Chapel Hill Street, and almost immediately, turn right onto Foster Street. The Durham Civic

Center and the Marriott Hotel are on the left. The sidewalk in the next 2 blocks after you cross Morgan Street is broken in several places but is still very walkable—just watch your step.

►Turn left onto Corporation Street. Down the hill on the right is the historic Durham Athletic Park where you began your walk.

Walk 14
Duke Chapel and Sarah P. Duke Gardens

General location: The most famous places on Duke's West Campus are featured on this walk: the chapel, the gardens, and the medical center.

Special attractions: The Sarah P. Duke Gardens, Duke Chapel, Duke's quads, Duke Divinity School, and the world-famous Duke University Medical Center.

Difficulty rating: Easy, packed dirt in the garden with some slight hills and flat, paved sidewalk to the chapel and the medical center.

Distance: 1.5 miles.

Walk 14

Estimated time: 45 minutes.

Services: An information kiosk near the steps that lead into the garden at the Anderson Street entrance offers more information about the gardens. For 25 cents, you can purchase a map of the entire gardens. Accessible restrooms are near the Terraced Gardens, and water fountains can be found in several locations. Emergency phone boxes are available in the gardens.

Restrictions: Dogs must be leashed and droppings picked up. Flowers and plants should be left for everyone to enjoy. Bicycling and team sports are not permitted in the gardens.

Steps from the garden to the chapel and on the campus part of the walk make the chapel part of the tour inaccessible to those in wheelchairs. Parts of the garden also are inaccessible, but you will be given alternate routes. Labels for plants are easily visible for those in wheelchairs.

For more information: Contact Duke Chapel, Duke University Medical Center, or Sarah P. Duke Gardens.

Getting started: This walk begins at the rose garden near the main gate of the Sarah P. Duke Gardens on Anderson Street. From I–85, take exit 174A, and go south on Hillandale Road. After crossing the Durham Freeway, Hillandale Road becomes Fulton Drive. Continue on Fulton Drive until you come to Erwin Road; turn left and then turn right onto Anderson Street. You will see the main entrance to the gardens on the right. Turn right at this entrance; free parking, including wheelchair-accessible parking, is available for visitors to the gardens. Walk through the main gate and down the steps to the rose garden.

Public transportation: Durham Area Transit Authority (DATA) bus 6 will take you to Flowers Drive. Get off the

Duke Chapel and Sarah P. Duke Gardens

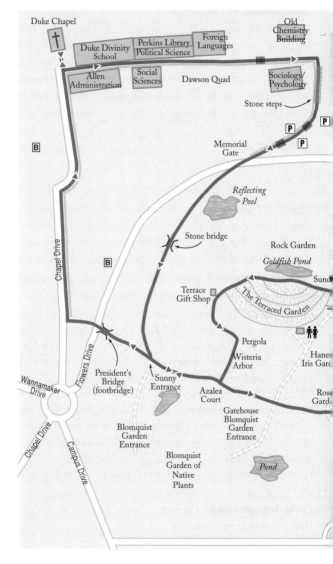

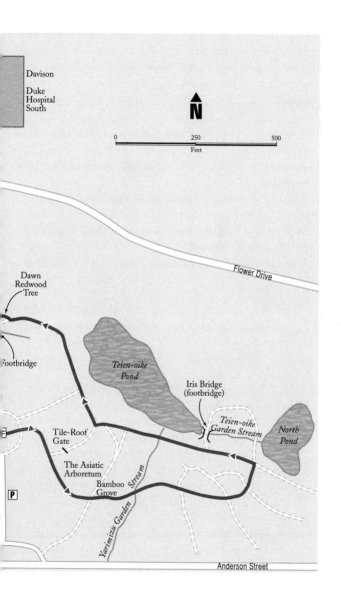

bus at this stop and walk through the garden to the rose garden, which is the starting point for this walk. The walk directions intersect with Flowers Drive, so you can start this walk from the bus stop and loop back.

Overview: Two memorable sights await you on this walk, one of which is Duke Chapel. Its soaring spires and English Gothic architecture will make you think you are in Old-World Europe rather than modern-day North Carolina. The word *masterpiece* springs to mind when one sees the chapel.

In 1925 James Buchanan Duke shared his dream of a splendid chapel with others. He and William Preston Few, president of Trinity College (later to become Duke University), were looking for a site for the new university. Duke told Few of his dream to have a church centrally located on the new campus that would dominate every other building.

Duke's dream was realized in the Duke University Chapel, which dominates not only the campus but also the city itself. As you ride through parts of west Durham, you will catch glimpses of the spires above the canopy of green in this city of trees.

The other equally magnificent sight on this walk is the Sarah P. Duke Gardens. They lie at the foot of the chapel, and when you are there you will momentarily forget you are on a busy, urban university campus.

The gardens began life in a former dumping ground for construction debris on the new West Campus. Plans were to construct a lake in the ravine, but declining budgets delayed this. Dr. Frederic Hanes, chief of the new University Medical Center and avid gardener with a love for the iris, had the idea of planting a garden as he walked by the site daily on his way to work. He mentioned his idea to Sarah

Visitors enjoy the fountains and foliage at the Sarah P. Duke Gardens.

P. Duke, widow of one of the university's founders, Benjamin N. Duke, and she decided to plant the garden.

Things did not go smoothly at first. For example, the gardens flooded several times, causing the gardeners to have to start over. However, the gardens were eventually established. After Sarah P. Duke's death, her daughter Mary Duke Biddle decided to complete the gardens in honor of her mother.

Admission to the gardens is free; however, donations are accepted and can be left in a box at the main gate; suggested donation is $3.00. The gardens are open every day of the year. Duke Chapel is open daily except Christmas Day; call ahead for daily schedules of special events.

The Walk

Your walk begins in the rose garden of the Sarah P. Duke Gardens. Throughout the gardens, benches provide places to stop, rest, and savor the sights. You will also see statuary interspersed among plants and trees.

►From the rose garden, take the path to your right when your back is to the steps that lead to the Anderson Street entrance.

You will see an arch straight ahead; this is the Kawarmon, or Tile-Roof Gate, the main gate into the twenty-acre Asiatic arboretum, the most recent addition to the gardens.

►Just before you reach the Tile-Roof Gate, turn right onto the gravel road that parallels the wooden fence. If you are in a wheelchair, take care as you ascend this small hill.

At the top of the knoll, four unmarked paths come together.

➤Veering slightly to your left, follow the path downhill through a bamboo grove toward the Japanese maple collection. Look for ducks as you cross Yarimizu Garden Stream.

➤After you exit the bamboo grove, several paths veer off to the left and right; stay on the path you are on until you reach the North Pond, which you will see as you emerge from the wooded area.

➤In front of the North Pond, turn left. You are walking alongside Teien-oike Garden Stream, which connects North Pond and the Teien-oike Garden pond, both on your right.

The bridge to your right before the pond is the Ayame-bashi, or Iris Bridge. You will see Duke University Medical Center on the right just beyond the garden pond.

➤As you near the tip of the garden pond and just before you reach the Tile-Roof Gate, angle to the right, going deeper into the gardens.

➤Follow the path to the left at the next intersection. You are heading toward the Hanes Iris Garden and the Terraced Gardens. Quiet, semiprivate areas open up into broader vistas in this part of the gardens. As you walk, read some of the many identifying labels of the plants that catch your eye. This section of the gardens is marked by wide, sloping lawns, and if you walk in summer, you may see people on blankets reading or otherwise enjoying the sunshine or the early twilight hours.

➤At the bottom of this slight decline, veer slightly right at the sign for the Dawn Redwood Tree, a huge old tree from China. Or you may choose to cross the footbridge to your left and see the sundial; if you do, return to this point and go left after you view the sundial. Straight across the path on the right is a Japanese cedar and a bench. Just ahead on the right is a water fountain and bench. At the water fountain, look left at the Terraced Gardens.

➤Walkers can turn right at the first intersection just past the water fountain and see the rock garden and a small goldfish pond covered in water lilies. The rock garden is not accessible to wheelchairs. If you walk through the rock garden, resume the walk from this point.

The Terraced Gardens are the heart of the gardens. Festive ceremonies, including weddings, often take place on the lawns near the terraces. Beyond the terraces you will see the often-photographed Wisteria Garden and pergola.

➤Enter the Terraced Gardens on your left at the far entrance, and follow the dirt path to the Terrace Shop, the garden gift shop. A small "shop" sign marks this entrance.

➤Those on foot may choose to walk through the Terraces on any of the designated paths and to the Wisteria Arbor.

Note: For those in wheelchairs, the Wisteria Arbor is inaccessible from the Terraced Gardens, so use the following directions to access the Wisteria Arbor: Turn left at the shop and go through the Terraced Gardens to the restrooms. Take the path beside the restrooms to the right, leading away from the Terraced Gardens and up the incline. At the next intersection of paths, turn right and travel about 20 feet to another intersection of paths at the gatehouse entrance to the H. L. Blomquist Garden of Native Plants. Turn right at this intersection, and follow the path back to the Wisteria Garden on your right. Both walkers and those in wheelchairs should now be in front of the Wisteria Arbor.

Walk inside the arbor, take a seat on one of the benches, and relax. The marker in the center commemorates Mary

Duke Biddle's gift of the gardens in memory of her mother, Sarah P. Duke, with the inscription, IN WHOSE LIFE WERE BLENDED THE STRENGTH OF THE SOUL AND THE BEAUTY OF FLOWERS. You will have a good view of the terraces from this perspective.

►Return to the path in front of the Wisteria Arbor and enter the circle called Azalea Court in front of the sculpture. Note the Dogwood Medallion and the inscription from English essayist Francis Bacon: GOD ALMIGHTY FIRST PLANTED A GARDEN, AND, INDEED, IT IS THE PUREST OF HUMAN PLEASURES.

Entrances to the H. L. Blomquist Garden of Native Plants are to the right and to the left from the sculpture. For those in wheelchairs, the best path to the Blomquist Garden is to the left of the sculpture bearing the Bacon quotation at the gatehouse entrance. If you wish to visit the Blomquist Garden, do so now.

The H. L. Blomquist Garden of Native Plants contains an excellent collection of wildflowers, two bog ponds, a collection of carnivorous plants unique to North Carolina, and more than 900 species and varieties of plants. Visit the Blomquist pavilion, a garden shelter with an antique slate roof beside a small pond.

From the Blomquist Garden, return to the Azalea Court and Dogwood Medallion circle.

►Facing the Wisteria Arbor, turn left along the path leading away from Azalea Court and Dogwood Medallion. Ahead is Sunny Entrance and the President's Bridge.

Wheelchair users, please note: This is the end of the accessible portion of this walk. Turn back through the Azalea Court and go to the rose garden. Enter the circle in the rose garden and turn right, going up the ramp to the garden exit.

➤To continue to Duke Chapel, go up the steps at Sunny Entrance and cross the President's Bridge, a wooden-surface bridge with stone columns.

➤Cross Flowers Drive at the pedestrian crossing.

➤Take the paved pathway on the other side of this street to Chapel Drive.

➤Turn right and walk toward the chapel, noticing the Duke banners and motto "Knowledge and Faith."

At the circular drive, look at the chapel and the bells in the chapel tower.

➤Follow the sidewalk to the right around the circular drive. The first building to the right is the Allen Administration Building.

Of Interest

The Bell Tower and Carillon

Duke endowment members George G. Allen and William R. Perkins donated the carillon to the university. The fifty bells were cast in England and brought to the chapel tower in 1932. The largest at 11,200 pounds measures almost 7 feet at the mouth and the smallest weighs 10 pounds and is 8 inches across.

The hunchback of Notre Dame would not be swinging the bell ropes in this belfry. Instead, he would work in a room below the carillon and use a hand clavier, which controls the clappers. Bell recitals are at 5:00 P.M. weekdays and before and after Sunday services.

The statue in the middle of the lawn is of James B. Duke, a university founder. The cigar he holds suggests Duke wasn't concerned about the dangers of smoking.

Duke Chapel's impressive spires.

The world-famous Duke Divinity School is the last building on your right before you reach the chapel.

At the doors of the chapel, examine the portal. Several sculptured figures are above and inside the portal, including Thomas Coke, an English Methodist missionary and bishop. Inside the portal also are sculptures of Girolamo Savonarola, a Dominican preacher; Martin Luther, German theologian and reformer; John Wycliffe, martyred for his English translation of the Bible; and John Wesley, founder of Methodism. To the right are sculptures of Thomas Jefferson, Robert E. Lee, and Sidney Lanier, a Southern poet.

Inside the chapel, look at the stained-glass windows with their depictions of characters and stories from the Bible. More than 300 of the figures in the stained-glass windows are life size. The chapel seats 1,500 people and the choir seats 150.

➤As you leave the chapel, follow the sidewalk to your left.

➤In front of Duke Divinity School, at the streetlight and bench, just before you reach the bus stop, turn left and follow the sidewalk on Dawson Quad. The Divinity School, Perkins Library, the political science department, and the foreign languages department are housed in one large building on the left of the quad.

Allen Administration, the Social Sciences Building, and the Sociology and Psychology Building are on your right along Dawson Quad. Duke Hospital South is in Davison, which is ahead of you.

➤Facing Davison, turn right and walk on a flagstone path bordered by boxwoods. As you walk by Davison, notice the structure's contrasting architecture. Here you can see the growth of the Duke medical community by observing

Of Interest

Duke and Durham, the City of Medicine

Durham proudly, perhaps justifiably, claims the title City of Medicine, USA. The largest and fastest-growing industry in Durham is medicine and healthcare. Durham has more than 2,000 physicians, with a physician-to-population ratio five times the national average. With 1,500 hospital beds, Durham boasts a bed-to-population ratio twice the national average.

Research Triangle Park in Durham County is home to seventy research and development companies; many are in health-related areas.

Four modern hospitals make their home in Durham: North Carolina Eye & Ear Hospital, Durham Regional, Veterans Affairs Medical Center, and Duke University Medical Center. The medical center, the third largest teaching hospital in the country, employs 13,500 people, and is a leader in several fields, including AIDS, heart, cancer, and arthritis research.

The Duke University School of Medicine ranks near the top of the medical schools in the United States, and competition for admission is intense. In 1993, 6,000 applicants competed for one hundred openings.

how Duke Hospital South was enlarged from the original Gothic structure of Davison to its more modern addition.

➤The stone path ends at the entrance to a parking area. Pick up the sidewalk that runs parallel to this parking area and follow it until it ends near an emergency telephone box. You will see a set of steps beside the phone box.

➤Follow these steps down to another gated parking lot.

➤Turn right, and cross the parking lot. At the gate at the opposite end of this parking lot, look for the lamppost and another flight of steps.

➤Walk down these steps and then to a marked pedestrian crossing on Flowers Drive.

➤Cross Flowers Drive and enter the gardens at Memorial Gate.

➤Inside the garden, stay on the path to the right. Ahead of you is a stone bridge; the Reflecting Pool is on your left, and a stone wall is on your right. At the next fork, you will see the President's Bridge to your right.

➤Veer left and walk past the phone box straight through Azalea Court.

Notice the arches for climbing plants along this part of the path. To the right is the gate house, one of the entrances to the H. L. Blomquist Garden of Native Plants. You are now approaching the rose garden.

➤Go to the right around the rose garden; just ahead you will see the stone steps bordered by stone ramps. Walk up the steps and follow the path out of the gardens through the Gothic gate to the parking area where you began your walk.

Walk 15
Duke Forest

General location: The walk begins beside the Washington Duke Inn and Golf Club and loops around the hotel's golf course through an urban forest.

Special attractions: Washington Duke Inn and Golf Club, Duke Cross-Country Trail, and Fit Loop.

Difficulty rating: Moderate, with hard-packed dirt surface of gravel and rock dust with several hills.

Distance: The Duke trail is a 2.9-mile loop; the Fit Trail Loop is 0.8 mile for a total of 3.7 miles.

Estimated time: 2 hours.

Services: Parking, emergency phone boxes every 0.5 mile, restrooms at the Washington Duke Inn, water fountain at the end of the cross-country trail. Maps are posted at major entrances to the trail.

Duke Forest

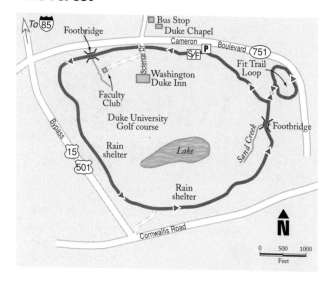

Restrictions: Enter only at gated roads. Do not walk after sunset; walk with a partner; stay off the golf course. Bikers must yield to pedestrians, stay on the gravel trail, warn when passing, control speed, and watch for leashed dogs. Helmets are recommended. No motorized vehicles are permitted. No fires, hunting, shooting, or overnight camping. Do not disturb vegetation. Leash dogs. Water is available at the inn and at the end of the trail loop; carry water with you in the summer.

For more information: Contact the Washington Duke Inn and Golf Club or the Office of Duke Forest.

Getting started: This walk begins near Washington Duke Inn at the gravel parking lot for the Duke Cross-Country Trail. From I–85, take exit 174, which is by-pass 15/501, and go south. Go about 1 mile and exit east onto Cameron Boulevard, which is also NC 751. Go approximately 0.3 mile, and you will come to the intersection with Science Drive. Duke University is on your left; to your right is the Washington Duke Inn. Go approximately 0.1 mile on Cameron Boulevard and park in the gravel lot.

Public transportation: Durham Area Transit Authority (DATA) bus 6 goes to Duke Chapel. If you walk behind the chapel you will be on Science Drive, which intersects with Cameron Boulevard about 0.5 mile down the road. Turn left onto Cameron Boulevard, walk about a block, and you will be at the gravel parking lot where the walk begins.

Overview: In the 1920s, Duke University began buying small farms and forests to act as a buffer for the new campus, then under construction. These wooded tracts also encouraged forestry education. Dr. Clarence F. Korstian became manager of the newly acquired lands, totaling 4,696 acres, and he also became the first dean of the Duke School of Forestry in 1938. Dr. Korstian used the proceeds from the sale of forest products to acquire more land.

Dr. Korstian accomplished many goals with the land. He successfully demonstrated timber management techniques, developed an experimental forest for research, and provided an outdoor laboratory for forestry students. The lands have had much wider purposes, helping to expand knowledge in such fields as ecology and environmental science. Today Duke Forest totals 7,700 acres, in six divisions covering parts of four counties. Duke Forest makes Duke University unique because it is such a valuable research tool so near campus.

The Duke Cross-Country Trail and Fit Loop is a popular recreational facility, and once you walk on this beautiful trail you will understand why. You will enjoy this trail almost any season of the year. In May you can enjoy the fragrance of honeysuckle; in the fall, the leaves of the hardwoods are beautiful. Even a winter walk can be lovely because Durham rarely gets snow—the average temperature in the Triangle area year-round is 70° F—but a winter walk might reward you with snow or ice-tipped pines.

This heavily used trail is popular with walkers, joggers, and those who simply like to take a leisurely walk in the woods. You might see parents pushing babies in strollers, nature lovers, and birders. If you are a bird watcher, take your field guide. You will see many of the birds native to this area, such as cardinals, mockingbirds, eastern bluebirds, and Carolina chickadees.

Although recreational use of Duke Forest is limited, many tracts do have hiking trails. Picnicking is available at some of these tracts of forestland. Contact the Office of Duke Forest for information.

The Walk

Note: If you want to walk only the shorter Fit Trail Loop, turn left from the parking lot and walk about 0.5 mile. Signs will direct you to the Fit Trail Loop.

➤From the gated parking area, turn right and begin walking on the Duke Cross-Country Trail. You will quickly enter a heavily wooded area. Soon you will come to Science Drive. To take a short excursion through the Washington Duke Inn, turn left and follow the sidewalk along Science Drive to the inn.

➤Return to where you left the trail on Science Drive.

➤Turn left onto the trail. Although you are walking parallel to busy Cameron Boulevard, you will probably see squirrels, rabbits, or other wildlife along the trail.

The Fit Trail Loop is a popular walking and exercise spot on Duke University's campus.

The Washington Duke Inn and Golf Club:
Elegance and History

The Washington Duke Inn was Durham's first deluxe hotel, and today it has the distinction of being the region's only four-star hotel. The elegant facade you see as you walk toward the entrance entices you to walk in and take a closer look at this beautiful inn.

Inside, examine the elegant lobby and the portrait of Washington Duke hanging behind the concierge's desk. At the entrance to the Fairview Restaurant in the lobby, notice the plate depicting the Semans-Duke family emblem.

Perhaps the most striking feature of this inn is the history that awaits you as you turn left along the hall in the lobby in the form of photographs, furniture, articles of clothing, medals, and other treasures of the Duke family. The heirlooms along this hallway create a revealing picture of the late 1800s and 1900s and of the life of this famous family.

Numerous photographs and portraits hang along the hallway. Many of these are formal, showing serious men and women. Some, however, are more casual, such as the ones showing the Duke children playing at the seashore.

Washington Duke's rolltop desk from his office at the Bull Factory of the American Tobacco Company is at the end of the hall, along with some Duke children's formal and informal dresses. Busts of several of the Dukes, including James Buchanan Duke, Washington Duke, Benjamin Newton Duke, and Angier Buchanan Duke line the hallway.

Angier Biddle Duke served as U.S. ambassador to El Salvador, Spain, Denmark, and Morocco. The wall display of his flag, medals, and keys to cities presented to him and other family members takes you to places around the globe and provides a sense of the Duke family's influence in North Carolina, the nation, and the world.

Dresses worn by Sarah Pearson Angier Duke, including her 1877 wedding dress and her fifteenth anniversary celebration dress, are displayed at the end of the hall.

Along the way, look at the pines, oaks, maples, and poplars that make up this forest. Frequently the leaves and branches form canopies over the trail, which help to make the walk cooler on hot summer days.

You will get glimpses of the fairways of the golf course through a small stand of trees to the left. Notice the undergrowth along this trail, including beautiful ferns; don't touch the poison ivy.

A rain shelter to the left is easily accessible, should you need it. Park benches provide quiet spots where you can look out at the golf course, lakes, and fountains. Hills along this section of the trail are fairly short and easy to navigate. Ahead is such a hill, and at the bottom of the hill a footbridge crosses a small stream.

You will come to another emergency phone box, map, and a trail that forks back to the right. This trail connects the cross-country trail and Cornwallis Road. Stay on the trail.

You will come to another hill, which is the steepest incline on the trail. At the top, look to your left for a good view of the golf course and the lake. Another emergency rain shelter is close by.

You have left the Cornwallis Road traffic noise behind. To your right is residential housing. Past the aboveground sewer line you will come to the junction with the trail that connects you to the Fit Trail Loop.

➤To take the Fit Trail Loop, go straight; if you wish to continue on the cross-country trail, turn left and cross the footbridge.

The Fit Trail Loop is a relatively flat, hard-packed surface with a few patches of loose rock. At the beginning of the loop, read the Total Fitness Board. This guide will help you find your target heart rate.

➤Turn right, go past the emergency phone box on your left, and begin this portion of the loop.

Along the way, you will see exercise directional boards for the Fit Trail. These information boards suggest toning exercises you can do along the fitness trail, and alongside you will see equipment to help you do the sit-ups, push-ups, chin lifts, and other exercises. When you finish, you will see a sign congratulating you on completing the Fit Trail.

➤Turn right at the phone box and walk back to the cross-country trail.

➤Turn right, cross the footbridge, and continue along the trail. The golf course is on your left, and the Washington Duke Inn is ahead.

A water fountain is just ahead and up the hill. The trail is usually slightly washed out here, so watch your footing.

➤Go through the gate to the graveled parking lot, which is where you began the walk. If you are taking the bus at Duke Chapel, continue on the trail to the intersection of Science Drive and Cameron Boulevard; turn right, cross the boulevard, and walk back to the bus stop in front of the chapel.

Walk 16
Research Triangle Park

General location: Walk a portion of the perimeter of one of the world's premier research parks. This walk takes you by beautifully landscaped research centers bordering a densely wooded area.

Special attractions: Urban park scenes, modern architecture of the famous research labs of various corporations.

Difficulty rating: Moderate, a few hills, mostly on asphalt with some short, unpaved sections.

Distance: 6.5 miles.

Estimated time: 3.5 hours.

Services: Restrooms and water during business hours on the main floor and on the downstairs floor of the Robert M. Hanes Memorial Building.

Research Triangle Park

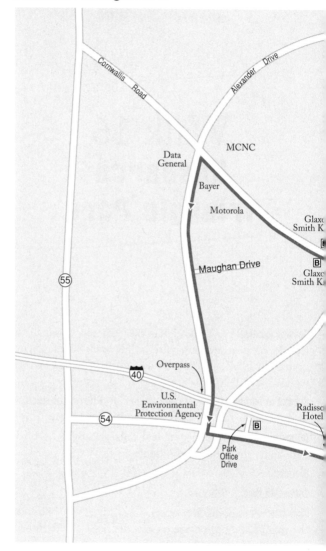

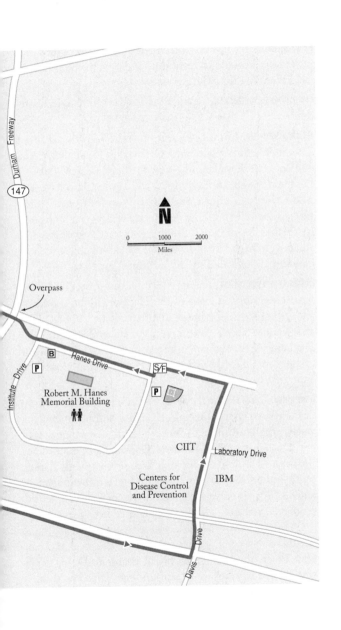

Restrictions: Dogs must be leashed and their droppings picked up. Water and restrooms available to the public in the Hanes building during business hours.

For more information: Contact the Research Triangle Foundation.

Getting started: From I–40, exit on NC 55 north. In about 1.75 miles, turn right onto Cornwallis Road where you will see a sign welcoming you to the Research Triangle Park and a sign for Institute Drive. Turn right onto Institute Drive and almost immediately turn left onto Hanes Drive. The only building on this short drive is the Robert M. Hanes Memorial Building. Park in the parking area adjacent to the softball fields and volleyball courts located past the Hanes building on Institute Drive.

Public transportation: Triangle Transit Authority (TTA) Orange Line stops in front of the Hanes building mornings and afternoons. For buses at other times, contact TTA and inquire about shuttle service. From Durham, take Durham Area Transit Authority (DATA) Bus 12 and transfer to TTA Orange Line at the Radisson Governors Inn.

Overview: The Research Triangle Park is the heart of the triangle formed by Raleigh's North Carolina State University, the University of North Carolina at Chapel Hill, and Durham's Duke University. Consisting of 6,800 acres, the park is limited to research and development. Almost one hundred such corporations and government agencies and 3,700 employees in the park make it a world-renowned research and development center.

When you visit the park, you will be amazed at what is *not* there. No conglomeration of high-rise steel and concrete greets the eye. Urban blight is absent. Do not envision dark, dusty labs in dreary buildings when you think of the research park. Instead, picture beautifully landscaped lawns gracing architecturally stunning buildings.

There is no huge grand entrance. In fact, visitors frequently inquire about the location of the main entrance, apparently wishing to have their picture taken by some imaginary massive gate.

Actually, the park has no singular focal point. Instead, it looks just like its name: beautifully landscaped grounds with green lawns and natural settings. Buildings are nestled in pine groves, often fronted by a reflecting lake. Pansies, mums, jonquils, tulips, azaleas, and irises line the drives in spring and summer, accenting the natural areas that make up the park and creating perfect places to bike, run, and jog. Spring is an especially beautiful time to visit; the sandy soil and temperate climate make it ideal for azaleas, which create profuse masses of white, pink, and red flowers.

Even the park's signage is tastefully done. Small well-landscaped entrance signs are the norm for the organizations that make their home in the park; you access these entrances via wide streets identified by attractive burgundy signs.

A 6-mile asphalt trail, used regularly by walkers, joggers, bikers, and inline skaters, circles the heart of the park, and more miles of trail are planned.

The Walk

➤From the parking lot at the softball courts, cross Institute Drive and go onto the jogging trail that parallels Hanes Drive.

➤At the end of Hanes Drive, cross Institute Drive. You are now walking alongside Cornwallis Road.

The overpass across NC 147 (Durham Freeway) has pedestrian markings and has been widened to accommodate walkers, bikers, and joggers. Use care while crossing the overpass.

Just past the overpass is a stoplight. On both sides of Cornwallis Road, you can see the buildings of Glaxo Smith Kline. These award-winning buildings, some of the most famous in the park, were built in 1972. The building on your left is a compilation of poured concrete modules stacked in a seemingly random fashion. Notice the angled structural columns of the building. All structural columns and even the flagpole are 22.5 degrees off vertical. This was the site of the movie *Brainstorm*.

Ahead on your left, look at the beautifully landscaped grounds with river birch, oak, and pine trees. This is the home of Motorola. The main building is a series of intersecting rectangles, each of which is a different height of either one, two, three, or four stories.

Notice the modernistic, angled facade that highlights the front of the Microelectronics Center of North Carolina (MCNC) on the right. MCNC is a private nonprofit corporation in partnership with the North Carolina universities, businesses, and state government. It supports research, education, and technology in microelectronics, communications, and supercomputing, and a CRAY Y-MP supercomputer housed here is the largest in the Southeast.

➤Turn left at the stop sign at the intersection of Cornwallis Road and Alexander Drive, just past Motorola. You are now walking beside Alexander Drive. Data General is on your right.

On the left, the eight stories of tinted glass of the Bayer Building beautifully reflect the pine grove in front of the building. This structure's most distinctive feature is the black pentagon-shaped, six-story decorative flying buttress on the right side.

►Cross I–40, following the pedestrian markings on the overpass. The large brick complex on your right is part of the U.S. Environmental Protection Agency that makes its home in the research park.

►Turn left onto NC 54. Just after you cross the footbridge, you will see the Radisson Governors Inn, banks, and other small businesses to your left. The DATA has a transfer point here and Triangle Transit Authority (TTA) has a terminal here.

►At the next intersection, turn left so that you are walking beside Davis Drive. The Centers for Disease Control and Prevention are housed in the large sprawling complex on the left. This is also home to the National Center for Health Statistics, Public Health Services, and the U.S. Department of Health and Human Services.

Adjacent to this building is CIIT, the Chemical Industry Institute of Toxicology. The dark beige brick building has wide, sloping lawns accented with pines, oaks, and crepe myrtles. On the right, the beige two-story brick building fronted with wide lawns is the IBM complex.

►Turn left onto Cornwallis Road and follow the path down the hill.

►After walking about 0.1 mile, turn left onto Institute Drive at the sign for park information. You are now back at your starting point.

Walk 17
Tar Heels and Franklin Street

General location: The University of North Carolina at Chapel Hill as well as Franklin Street, the main street in the town of Chapel Hill.

Special attractions: Franklin Street with its interesting shops, Ackland Art Museum, Coker Arboretum, the Memorial Bell Tower, Kenan Memorial Stadium, the Dean Smith Center, and the Carolina Inn.

Difficulty rating: Easy; a few hills; all-brick sidewalk except for Franklin Street and the walk to the Smith Center, which are concrete.

Distance: 4 miles.

Estimated time: 2 hours.

Tar Heels and Franklin Street

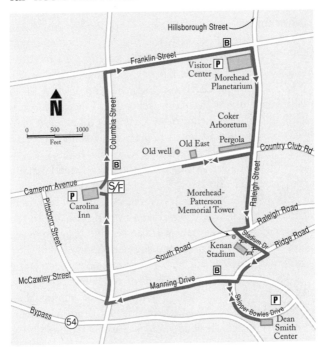

Services: Restrooms at the hotel, in the museum, and in several campus buildings when open. Food at the hotel, along Franklin Street, at Chase Cafeteria, and at the University Student Center when they are open. Emergency phone boxes are located at regular intervals on the campus.

Restrictions: Dogs must be leashed and droppings picked up. Ackland Art Museum is closed Mondays and Tuesdays.

For more information: Contact the visitor center at the university or the Chapel Hill Chamber of Commerce.

Getting started: This walk begins at the Carolina Inn at 211 Pittsboro Street. To reach the hotel from I–40/85, take NC 54 south toward Chapel Hill. In about 15 minutes, you will come to Carrboro, North Carolina. Stay on bypass NC 54 through Carrboro; Carrboro and Chapel Hill's boundaries are adjacent to each other. Once in Chapel Hill, follow signs to downtown Chapel Hill and exit onto Columbia Street. Follow it to Cameron Avenue, and turn left on this one-way street; the Carolina Inn is on your left. Take the next left, which is Pittsboro Street; parking for guests is in a lot on the left.

If you are not staying at the inn, look for metered street parking. You may ask permission to park your car in the inn's parking lot while you walk; depending upon availability, the staff may let you use their parking lot. If their guest parking lot is full, go back to Columbia Street, going toward downtown, and turn right onto Franklin Street. Morehead Planetarium is on the right at number 250. Metered parking is available in this lot; if the visitor center is open, you can obtain a guest parking pass there.

Public transportation: Bus stops are located along Columbia Street in front of the inn (buses D, G, N, S, and T). Buses C, D, J, N, S, and T stop on Pittsboro Street. Contact Chapel Hill Transit for times, fares, and accessibility and for information on connections to the Raleigh airport as well as Raleigh (CAT) and DATA buses.

Overview: Come walk America's oldest state university campus. As you walk down Franklin Street and along the campus streets, you may learn why many alumni, friends of the university, citizens of the small town, and others have nicknamed Chapel Hill the Southern Part of Heaven.

Walk 17

Chapel Hill was named for New Hope Chapel, a small Episcopal church, which stood on a hill in what was then a forest at the intersection of two of the county's primary roads. This location is now the site of the Carolina Inn. In 1793 the first town lots were auctioned some four years after the university was chartered.

Life in the early years of the university was spartan. The cornerstone for Old East, the university's first building, was laid October 12, 1793. Most of the university activity—dorm as well as academic life—occurred in Old East. At one time, fifty-six students occupied fourteen rooms in the building. It was difficult to study in such conditions, so students went into the forest surrounding Old East and erected study huts—quiet places where they could study in peace. For a while, an acceptable excuse for being unprepared for class was the weather. If the roofs of the study huts leaked or if the weather was too cold, a student could be excused for being unprepared for class.

Today Old East is on the National Register of Historic Places and is the oldest state university building in the nation. You will pass this historic building on your walk and see for yourself that the forest that surrounded the building in those early years has been replaced by many more university buildings.

The town of Chapel Hill grew with the university. Franklin Street, named for Benjamin Franklin, became the center of commerce in the small town. Today the street offers a distinctive blend of restaurants, shopping, history, and nostalgia. Here you can purchase university memorabilia as well as clothes from stylish boutiques or just sit and watch the people who crowd this street most hours of the day and late into the night. The eastern end of Franklin Street offers a collection of fine historic homes, many of which belonged at one time to university employees; some still belong to people connected to the university.

The school's enrollment has now increased to almost 25,000 students coming from one hundred North Carolina counties, forty-nine states, and more than one hundred foreign countries. The town of Chapel Hill has 45,000 residents, including professors, students, businesspeople, and retirees from all over the world. It is truly an incomparable place. Ask any friend or alumnus of the university and she or he will probably agree that Franklin Street is the road that leads to the Southern Part of Heaven.

The Walk

The walk begins at Cameron Avenue and Columbia Street in front of the sign for the Carolina Inn. Walk out any of the doors from the Carolina Inn and go to this intersection.

➤Cross Cameron Avenue.

➤Cross Columbia Street, and turn left, walking toward Franklin Street and downtown. A low stone wall bordering a small garden with stone picnic tables on your right is adjacent to Abernathy Hall, home of Extension and Continuing Education. The Frank Borden and Barbara Lasater Hanes Art Center is to the right of the Ackland Art Museum.

The Ackland museum exhibits Greek and Roman art, Western paintings and sculptures since the Middle Ages, African and Asian art, North Carolina folk art, and contemporary art.

Look across Columbia Street at the large bell in the wrought-iron display. It was removed from the First Baptist Church established in Chapel Hill in 1854 and is now

The Old Well is one of the most famous landmarks on UNC-Chapel Hill's campus.

on display adjacent to the University Baptist Church. You are now approaching one of the most famous intersections in North Carolina, the intersection of Columbia and Franklin Streets.

➤Turn right onto Franklin Street. Take time to browse in the coffee shops, restaurants, clothing stores, university memorabilia shops, and book and record shops along the street. Other than the Carolina Inn and a university cafeteria, this is the best place to obtain food on this walk.

This shopping area smoothly blends with the university. The first university building you will see is Battle Hall on the right. Completed in 1912, it was named for Kemp Battle, university president from 1876 to 1891.

Next to Battle Hall is McCorkle Place, a mall between Cameron and Franklin Streets. From Franklin Street, you can see the Civil War monument in the center of the mall.

Erected in 1913 by the North Carolina Division of the United Daughters of the Confederacy, the monument memorializes the 1,062 university alumni who joined the Confederate Army and the 362 of them who died in the Civil War. The monument depicts a young student, now a soldier, holding a rifle. The war indeed caused many students to leave the university and rush home to enlist. At one point the number of graduates left on campus was down to 4. Today, the monument is affectionately called Silent Sam. You will have an opportunity to visit more of the landmarks at McCorkle Place when you reach the Old Well.

➤Continue along Franklin Street. Morehead Planetarium is on the right at number 250. It is the first major planetarium owned by a university. Inside are the 330-seat Star Theater, exhibits, an art gallery, and a gift shop. American astronauts have been trained in celestial navigation in the planetarium, and the 35-foot walk-in model Copernican Orrery, demonstrating how planets revolve around the sun, is one of two in the world. Be sure to see the 14-foot pendulum of the Howard clock. The university visitor center in the planetarium's west wing is a good place to pick up brochures and to watch a brief video that provides an overview of the history of the university.

Outside the planetarium be sure to visit the hybrid-rose garden and see the sundial in the center of the garden. With a diameter of 35 feet, it is one of the largest sundials of its type.

On the right and next to the planetarium is Chapel of the Cross Episcopal Church. Noteworthy for its Gothic revival architecture, it is also the oldest church in Chapel Hill.

Pauli Murray was ordained in Chapel of the Cross in 1977. She was the first African-American woman ordained as a priest by the Episcopal Church in America. An interesting piece of her story is that her grandmother was baptized in the chapel of this same church in 1854 as a slave baby.

Across the street at the intersection of Raleigh, Hillsborough, and Franklin Streets at number 401 is the Phillips Law Office, Chapel Hill's first law office. A one-story Italian-style stucco cottage, the building was erected in the mid-1840s and restored in 1983.

►Turn right onto Raleigh Street. You will not see a sign for Raleigh Street here; to the left, across Franklin Street, this is called Hillsborough Street. Note the brick Spencer Residence Hall with black-shuttered windows at the corner of Raleigh and Franklin Streets.

The large yellow house with Doric columns and a two-story Corinthian portico on the left of Raleigh Street at

Of Interest

Coker Arboretum

Coker Arboretum, a five-acre naturalistic garden, sits in the middle of one of the busiest parts of the campus. Containing approximately 580 species of trees and shrubs, it is a quiet respite in the midst of the bustling university.

Dr. William Chambers Coker, the university's first professor of botany and the first chair of the university's building and grounds committee, developed this boggy field as an outdoor classroom for the study of trees, shrubs, and vines native to the state. Before this, the land was used as pasture for mules, cattle, and other animals belonging to university professors and staff.

After the land was developed as an outdoor classroom, Coker added trees and shrubs from other countries. Among the varieties you can enjoy in your walk through the arboretum are crepe myrtle, pine, Chinese pistachio, Japanese plum, yew, oak, elm, sweetgum, bald cypress, hawthorn, and gingko.

400 Franklin Street is the UNC president's house. The grounds of Coker Arboretum are just past Spencer hall on the right.

►Turn right onto Cameron Avenue and walk under the 200-foot pergola. Made of sturdy locust posts, the pergola is covered in wisteria, native yellow jasmine, and roses. Benches at each end of the pergola and inside the arboretum provide places to rest and appreciate the surroundings.

►Continue along Cameron Avenue. Davie Hall, home of the Department of Psychology, is on the right. Just beyond Davie Hall is New East. Before you reach this building, walk right and between New East and Davie Hall to view the Thomas Wolfe Memorial. An 850-pound bronze relief sculpture, it is, appropriately for Wolfe, of an angel and is inscribed with a line from Wolfe's most famous novel, *Look Homeward, Angel:* O LOST, AND BY THE WIND GRIEVED, GHOST, COME BACK AGAIN. Wolfe studied playwrighting in New East and graduated from the university in 1920.

➤Return to Cameron Avenue after visiting the sculpture.

Just ahead and on the right is Old East, the oldest state university building in the nation. Originally built in 1793, the building has undergone many renovations. In 1824 it was lengthened and a third story added. It was remodeled in 1848; the interior was remodeled in 1924.

The Old Well, the most recognizable university symbol and one of the most famous of the university's many famous landmarks, is ahead on the right. For years this was the sole water supply on campus; be sure to take a sip of water from the fountain in the center.

As you look away from Cameron Avenue at the site of the Old Well, you are again looking at the grounds of McCorkle Place, the mall between Cameron Avenue and Franklin Street you saw earlier in the walk. Straight ahead is a famous tree, the Davie poplar, and just beyond that is the Civil War monument you saw earlier. The Davie poplar is a tree that predates the university; many legends have grown up around the tree, and it has served as a rallying place on campus for almost 200 years.

Between the Davie poplar and Silent Sam is the Caldwell Monument. Joseph Caldwell, the university's first president, his wife, Helen Hogg Hooper, and her son by a previous marriage, Dr. William Hooper, are buried at the base of the white marble obelisk. Dr. Hooper is the grandson and namesake of William Hooper, one of the signers of the Declaration of Independence and was a university faculty member in ancient languages for many years. The Hooper residence is at 504 Franklin Street just beyond the president's home. For years it was tradition to pause and acknowledge the graves at commencement exercises as the graduation procession passed by.

The mall known as McCorkle Place is a wonderful place to stroll and study some of the history of the university. When you are ready to resume the walk, return to Cameron Avenue at the Old Well. Just beyond the Old Well is the building known as Old West.

➤Cross Cameron Avenue in front of Old West and walk back down the street. The campus YMCA is in front of you as you cross. Thomas Wolfe used an unheated room on the second floor of the YMCA as a quiet place to write.

To the left of the YMCA as you continue down Cameron Avenue is South Building. Originally a dormitory, its most famous resident was U.S. Pres. James K. Polk, class of 1818.

Just past South Building, the terra-cotta stucco of the home of the Carolina Playmakers will capture your attention. Built in 1851 in the Greek revival style, it was originally a library and ballroom. Later it was the home of agricultural chemistry and then law, before becoming the home of dramatic art in 1925. In 1974 it was registered as a National Historic Landmark. Walk to the front of the building. Notice the Corinthian capitals with the wheat and corn at the top. Architect Alexander Jackson Davis used these symbols rather than traditional acanthus leaves that usually ornament Corinthian columns to make the capitals distinctly American. One persistent legend is that this beautiful building was used as stables for Union troops' horses during the Civil War.

Walk 17

Beside the Playmakers building is the Carr Building. Built in 1889, it is named for Julian Shakespeare Carr of Durham, the advertiser responsible for creating the famous Bull Durham cigarette logo. His name is carved in the scrollwork above the building's main entrance.

►At the intersection of Cameron Avenue and Raleigh Streets, turn right onto Raleigh. Davis Library is ahead and on your right. The largest educational building in North Carolina, the library has room for 1.8 million volumes, covers three acres, has nine floors, and ten acres of floor space. It was named for Texan Walter R. Davis, a former member of the university's board of trustees.

►Turn right onto South Road, which is also NC 54. Robert Allison Fetzer Gymnasium, named for Chapel Hill's first director of physical education and athletics, is across South Road. The building's distinctive architecture won a national design prize. Inside are three gymnasiums, six squash courts, and fifteen handball and racquetball courts.

Daniels Building (student stores) is on the right. Here you can visit the Ram's Head Book Store and other shops, including snack bars. Restrooms are available here.

►Turn left onto Stadium Drive at the pedestrian crossing just past Daniels. You are facing the Morehead-Patterson Memorial Bell Tower. Built in 1931, it is 172 feet tall, with a twin-bell electronically controlled carillon.

Straight ahead along Stadium Drive are wooded areas with picnic tables; these are used for tailgate parties before games at Kenan Memorial Stadium, which is just ahead and on the right. The stadium is home to Tar Heel football games. With seating for 43,000, it is a popular gathering place for Tar Heel fans on fall afternoons. Halftime productions feature the Tar Heel marching band and

Rameses the Ram, the university mascot, whose curled horns are painted Tar Heel blue.

Across Stadium Drive are several residence halls including Carmichael and Teague. Look through the openings between these brick buildings and you can catch glimpses of the Carolina blue of Fetzer Field, a running track. Hill Alumni Center is on the right just beyond Kenan Stadium.

➤At the foot of the hill, turn right onto Ridge Road. You will see soccer fields on the left, and paralleling parking areas for Ramshead alumni and visitors on the right.

At the stop sign for Ridge Road and Manning Drive, look ahead for a good view of the white dome of the Dean Smith Center.

➤Cross Manning Drive. You are now on a sidewalk along Skipper Bowles Drive, the road that leads to the Dean Smith Center. Home of Tar Heel basketball, the Smith Center, or Dean Dome, as it is nicknamed by fans everywhere, has seating capacity for 21,444. You will pass the entrance to the Kenan-Flagler School of Business on the right. The Dean Dome is also home to tennis exhibitions, stage productions, concerts, and other events. It is one of the nation's largest on-campus arenas.

➤After your visit to the Smith Center, retrace your steps along Skipper Bowles Drive and turn left onto Manning Drive. Chase Cafeteria is on the right.

➤Just past the Chase Cafeteria and the bus stop, veer to the right of the small parking area to stay on the brick sidewalk.

You are now entering the University Hospital area. North Carolina Memorial Hospital, North Carolina Neurosciences Hospital, North Carolina Children's Hospital,

North Carolina Women's Hospital, and North Carolina Clinical Cancer Center are all either on or just off Manning Drive. At the time of the writing of this book, long-range construction was under way; chances are there will be construction going on in this area for many years to come. Watch your step and watch for broken sidewalk and muddy patches, even on the brick sidewalk, through this area. You will cross several unnamed drives leading to the various hospitals, parking lots, and parking garages; each of these drives has a stop sign for drivers turning onto Manning Drive, but check carefully at each of these drives before crossing.

➤At the intersection of Manning Drive and Columbia Street, veer right so that you are walking on sidewalk. The School of Public Health is in Rosenau Hall on the left, and the Health Sciences Library is on the right. The School of Pharmacy is on the left in Beard Hall, and the School of Nursing is just across the street.

➤Look to your right for a good view of the bell tower. Across the street from Sitterson Hall is the Carolina Inn, where you began the walk.

➤Cross Columbia Street at Cameron Avenue to return to the Carolina Inn.

Appendix A: Other Sights

You may enjoy several other attractions that are either in or near Raleigh or Durham. Although they do not involve much walking, they have been enjoyed by millions of tourists and local residents.

In Raleigh

Joel Lane House

Originally called Wakefield, Raleigh's oldest dwelling was built in the 1760s by Joel Lane, who sold 1,000 acres of land to the state of North Carolina in 1792 to establish a capital. The restored gambrel-roofed home is open for touring and costumed docents tell the story of the house and period gardens.

North Carolina Museum of Art

Painting and sculpture representing 5,000 years of artistic heritage are available for viewing at this museum. The exhibits change regularly, but permanent exhibits include Egyptian artifacts, European paintings, modern art, American paintings, and a Judaic gallery devoted to Jewish ceremonial art. Featured works are by Georgia O'Keeffe, Winslow Homer, Camille Pissaro, and Botticelli.

Raleigh Memorial Auditorium

Built in 1932 as a memorial to the World War I dead, this limestone neoclassical building with Doric columns is home to the North Carolina Symphony and the North Carolina Theater. It has recently undergone extensive renovations and is now the site of touring Broadway plays.

In Durham

Bennett Place

Site of the negotiation leading to the largest troop surrender of the Civil War, this pre–Civil War farm is a reconstructed farmhouse with outbuildings. Union general William T. Sherman and Confederate general Joseph E. Johnston met here in 1865 to negotiate the surrender. An interpretive center and museum provide additional historical information about this event.

Duke Homestead and Tobacco Museum

This is the original home of Washington Duke, who was a farmer for most of his life. The homestead provides a glimpse of life as it must have been in the 1800s when the Dukes lived and farmed here. The museum chronicles the world of tobacco and offers activities that demonstrate early tobacco farming techniques as well as tobacco manufacturing processes.

West Point on the Eno

This city park is located on the Eno River 6 miles north of downtown Durham and features a reconstructed 1778 working gristmill. You can purchase stone-ground meal and flour, as well as other items in the mill's store. A re-created nineteenth-century blacksmith shop is open and features demonstrations and classes in the art of blacksmithing. Picnic facilities, hiking trails, fishing, rafting, and a variety of natural history programs, craft workshops, and concerts are available.

Outside Chapel Hill

Historic Hillsborough

This was the site of the 1788 North Carolina Constitutional Convention where delegates demanded a bill of rights before they would ratify the U. S. Constitution. More than one hundred late eighteenth- and early nineteenth-century structures remain in the Hillsborough historic district. Visit the Alexander Dickson House, the last headquarters of the Confederacy, which now serves as the Orange County Visitor Center. The Regulator Marker marks the site where six Regulators were hanged on June 19, 1771. See the Burwell School, a Presbyterian school for women for several years; it is being restored.

Appendix B: Contact Information

The list below gives you the phone numbers and addresses of all the local attractions, museums, and shops mentioned in the book. Contact individual attractions, museums, or shops to confirm opening times, locations, and entrance fees.

The Greater Raleigh Convention and Visitors Bureau, the Durham Convention and Visitors Bureau, the Capital Area Visitor Center, and the Chapel Hill/Orange County Visitors Bureau have a wealth of information about Raleigh, Durham, Chapel Hill, and nearby attractions.

For your convenience, the visitors bureaus for the three towns are listed directly below. To find specific contact information for the places mentioned in this book, first locate the city section within this appendix and then the category you want. For example, the North Carolina Museum of History will appear in the section on Raleigh and then alphabetically with the category, Activities, Attractions, and Museums. In this appendix, the cities have been listed by size, with Raleigh appearing first within the list.

Note: The area code for Raleigh, Durham, and Chapel Hill is 919.

Greater Raleigh Convention and Visitors Bureau
421 Fayetteville Street Mall, Suite 1505
P.O. Box 1879
Raleigh 27602
Tourist information: 834–5900
Toll-free: (800) 849–8499
e-mail: www.raleighcvb.org
Web site: www.raleighcvb.org
8:30 A.M. to 5:00 P.M. Monday through Friday.

Capital Area Visitor Center
301 North Blount Street
Raleigh 27601
733–7456
8:00 A.M. to 5:00 P.M. Monday through Friday; 9:00 A.M. to 5:00 P.M. Saturday; 1:00 to 5:00 P.M. Sunday.
Free half-hour parking.

Durham Convention and Visitors Bureau
101 East Morgan Street
Durham 27701
667–0288
For a 24-hour recording of events and information and to request information, call 688–BULL or (800) 772–BULL
www.durham-nc.com
8:30 A.M. to 5:00 P.M. Monday through Friday; 10:00 A.M. to 2:00 P.M. Saturday. Free parking. The entrance is on Morgan in front of the Visitors Center.

Chapel Hill/Orange County Visitors Bureau
501 West Franklin Street, Suite 104
Chapel Hill 27516
968–2060 or (888) 968–2060
www.chocvb.org

Raleigh

Activities, Attractions, and Museums
Artspace
201 East Davie Street
Raleigh 27601
821–2787
www.artspace.citysearch.com
10:00 A.M. to 5:00 P.M. Tuesday through Saturday; 10:00 A.M. to 9:00 P.M. on the first Friday of each month. Studio hours vary.

Gallery hours: 11:00 A.M. to 2:00 P.M. Tuesday through Friday; 10:00 A.M. to 4:00 P.M. Saturday. Free admission.

Exploris
412 South Blount Street
Raleigh 27601
834–4040
www.exploris.org
Call for admission information and schedules.

Haywood Hall House and Gardens
211 New Bern Place
Raleigh 27601
832–8357 or 832–4158
Free with limited accessibility.
10:30 A.M. to 1:30 P.M. Thursday, March through December, or by appointment. Tours available.

JC Raulston Arboretum
North Carolina State University
4301 Beryl Road
Raleigh 27695
515–3132
8:00 A.M. to 8:00 P.M. daily
www.arb.ncsu.edu
Free admission.

Mordecai Historic Park
Wake Forest Road and Mimosa Street
Raleigh 27601
834–4844
10:00 A.M. to 4:00 P.M. Monday and Wednesday through Saturday; 1:00 to 4:00 P.M. Sunday; closed Tuesday and holidays.
Guided tours are available. One-hour tours begin on the hour. Admission fee.

North Carolina Executive Mansion

200 North Blount Street
Raleigh 27601
733–3456 (Capital Area Visitor Center)
Hours vary. Call for an appointment for a thirty-minute guided tour of the public rooms or for seasonal garden tours. Free.

North Carolina Museum of History

5 East Edenton Street
Raleigh 27602
715–0200
nchistory.dcr.state.nc.us/museums
9:00 A.M. to 5:00 P.M. Tuesday through Saturday; noon to 5:00 P.M. Sunday; closed Monday. Free.
Fee parking underneath the museum building; free on weekends. Wheelchair-accessible entrance off Jones Street at Fletcher Garden Plaza.

North Carolina State Archives

109 East Jones Street
Raleigh 27601
733–3952
8:00 A.M. to 5:30 P.M. Tuesday through Friday; 8:00 A.M. to 5:30 P.M. Saturday. Closed Sunday and Monday. Free admission.

North Carolina State Capitol

1 Edenton Street
Raleigh 27601
733–4994
www.att:dcr.state.nc.us/sections/capitol
8:00 A.M. to 5:00 P.M. Monday through Friday; 9:00 A.M. to 5:00 P.M. Saturday; 1:00 to 5:00 P.M. Sunday. Free admission.

North Carolina State Legislative Building
16 West Jones Street
Raleigh 27601
733–4111
www.ncga.state.nc.us
8:00 A.M. to 5:00 P.M. Monday through Friday; 9:00 A.M. to 5:00 P.M. Saturday; 1:00 to 5:00 P.M. Sunday. Free. Call in advance to schedule a thirty-minute guided tour.

North Carolina State Library
109 East Jones Street
Raleigh 27601
733–3270
http://statelibrary.dcr.state.nc.us
8:00 A.M. to 5:30 P.M. Monday through Friday; 9:00 A.M. to noon and 1:00 to 5:00 P.M. Saturday. Genealogy only on Saturday.

North Carolina State Museum of Natural Sciences
Bicentennial Plaza
P. O. Box 29555
Raleigh 27626
733–7450
www.naturalsciences.org
9:00 A.M. to 5:00 P.M. Monday through Saturday; 1:00 to 4:40 P.M. Sunday; closed on state holidays.

Oakwood Cemetery
701 Oakwood Avenue
Raleigh 27601
832–6077
8:00 A.M. to 6:00 P.M. daily in spring and summer (March through September), 8:00 A.M. to 5:00 P.M. daily in winter (October through February). Office hours: 7:00 A.M. to 4:00 P.M. Monday through Friday. Tours are available by appointment.

Raleigh Little Theater and Rose Garden
301 Pogue Street
Box 5637
Raleigh 27650
821–4579 (office)
821–3111 (box office)
www.mindspring.com/~rallittletheater
Box office is open from 9:00 A.M. to 5:00 P.M. Monday through Friday.

Sertoma Arts Center
1400 West Millbrook Road
Raleigh 27609
420–2329
9:00 A.M. to 10:00 P.M. Monday through Thursday; 9:00 A.M. to 3:00 P.M. Friday; 10:00 A.M. to 3:00 P.M. Saturday; closed Sunday. Closed Saturday, June through August.

City Parks

City of Raleigh Department of Parks and Recreation
P.O. Box 590
Raleigh 27602
890–3285
www. raleigh-nc.org

Lake Johnson Park
5600 Avent Ferry Road
Raleigh 27606
233–2121
Daily, sunrise to sunset.

Pullen Park
520 Ashe Avenue
Raleigh 27606
831–6468
Hours vary seasonally; contact the park office for schedules. Admission to the park is free; fee for some rides.

Shelley Lake
1400 W. Millbrook Road
Raleigh 27609
420–2331
Daily, sunrise to sunset.

County Parks
Blue Jay Point County Park
3200 Pleasant Union Church Road
Raleigh 27614
870–4330
www.web.co.wake.nc.us/parksrec/
8:00 A.M. to sunset, daily and weekends; call for seasonal closing times. Closed Thanksgiving, Christmas Eve, Christmas Day, New Year's Day.

Hotels
Sheraton Raleigh Capital Center Hotel
421 South Salisbury Street
Raleigh 27601
834–9900 or (800) 834–2105
www.sheratoncapital.com

William Thomas House Bed and Breakfast
530 North Blount Street
Raleigh 27601
755–9400 or (800) 653–3466
www.williamthomashouse.com
Full breakfast, private baths, in-room telephones.

Schools
North Carolina State University
Hillsborough Street
Raleigh 27695
www.ncsu.edu
University information: 515–2011
Disability services for students: 515–7653

Peace College
14 East Peace Street
Raleigh 27601
508–2000 or (800) PEACE–47
www.peace.edu

Saint Mary's School
900 Hillsborough Street
Raleigh 27601
839–4000 or (800) 948–2557
www.saint-marys.edu

Shopping
Cameron Village Shopping Center
1900 Cameron Street
Raleigh 27601
821–1350
10:00 A.M. to 6:00 P.M. Monday through Saturday.

City Market
Moore Square Art District
Downtown Raleigh at Blount and Martin Streets
856–8873
www.citymarket.citysearch.com

Transportation
Capital Area Transit
828–7228
Raleigh Transit Authority
Information line: 828–SCAT (7228); TTY (teletypewriter service) number available by calling North Carolina Relay (800) 735–2962 and requesting a connection to the CAT information line or the CAT connector dispatcher 832–5815.

Raleigh/Durham International Airport
I–40, exit 284B, Airport Boulevard
RDU information assistance: 840–2123

The Raleigh Trolley
828–7228
Raleigh Transit Authority
Shuttle available 11:30 A.M. to 2:00 P.M. Monday through
Friday. Fare charged.
Historic narrative tours available first and third Saturdays
monthly, noon to 4:00 P.M. Fare charged.

Wolfline Transit System
North Carolina State University
Hillsborough Street
Raleigh 27695
515–WOLF

Durham

Activities, Attractions, and Museums

Carolina Theatre
309 West Morgan
Durham 27701
Box office: 560–3030
For rental arrangements or information, call 560–3040
Parking available on Morgan Street.

Duke University

Duke Chapel
Chapel Drive
Durham 27708
681–1704
www.chapel.duke.edu
Closed Christmas Day.
When classes are in session during regular academic
terms, the chapel is open 8:00 A.M. to 10:00 P.M. At other

times, the chapel is open 8:00 A.M. to 8:00 P.M. The chapel may close for special services.

Office of Duke Forest
Duke Forest Resource Manager
Levine Science Research Center, Room A114
Duke University
Durham 27706
684–8111
8:00 A.M. to 5:00 P.M. Monday through Friday.
www.duke.edu

Duke University Medical Center
Erwin Road
Durham 27710
684–8111
www.mc.duke.edu

Duke University Museum of Art
Duke University East Campus, Campus Drive
Durham 27708
684–5135
www.duke.edu/web/duma/
9:00 A.M. to 5:00 P.M. Tuesday through Friday; 11:00 A.M. to 2:00 P.M. Saturday; 2:00 to 5:00 P.M. Sunday. Closed Monday and holidays. Free admission.

Sarah P. Duke Gardens
Duke University
Box 90341
Durham 27708-0341
684–3698
www.hr.duke.edu/dukegardens
For information about special tours for the physically handicapped, call 684–3698.
8:00 A.M. to dusk daily.

Duke Memorial United Methodist Church

504 West Chapel Hill Street
Durham 27701
683–3467

Durham Bulls Athletic Park

409 Blackwell Street
Durham 27701
For ticket information, call 956–2855.
Ballpark Corner, the souvenir shop, is open from 9:00 A.M.
to 5:00 P.M. Monday through Friday, and longer on game
days.
To order memorabilia, call (800) 849–2855.

Historic Durham Athletic Park

500 West Corporation Street
Durham 27701
680–3278

North Carolina Mutual Life Insurance Company

Mutual Plaza
411 West Chapel Hill
Durham 27701
682–9201
Tours can be arranged.

The Research Triangle Foundation

2 Hanes Drive
Research Triangle Park 27709
549–8181
Office hours: 8:30 A.M. to 5:00 P.M. weekdays.

Royall Center for the Arts

120 Morris Street
Durham 27701
560–2787
9:00 A.M. to 9:00 P.M. Monday through Saturday; 1:00 to
6:00 P.M. Sunday.
Closed on major holidays.

Ryan Research Center Institute of Parapsychology
402 North Buchanan Boulevard
Durham 27701
688–8241
Tours of labs can be arranged.

Hotels
Durham Hilton
3800 Hillsborough Road
Durham 27705
383–8033

Washington Duke Inn and Golf Club
3001 Cameron Boulevard
Durham 27706
490–0999 or (800) 443–3853
www.washingtondukeinn.com

Schools
Duke University
2138 Campus Drive
Durham 27708
For Duke information, call 684–8111, or look for numbers
of specific places on Duke's campus in this listing.
www.duke.edu

Shopping
Ballpark Corner
Durham Bulls Athletic Park
409 Blackwell Street
Durham 27701
687–6550

The Book Exchange
107 West Chapel Hill Street
Durham 27701
682–4662

Brightleaf Square
Morgan-Peabody Street Loop
Durham 27701
688–5311
11:00 A.M. to 6:00 P.M. Monday through Saturday.

Wellspring Grocery
621 Broad Street
Durham 27701
286–2290

Transportation

ABC Cab Company
682–0437

Brad's Airport Shuttle
493–5890

Duke University Transit
712 Wilkerson Avenue
Durham 27708
684–2218

Durham Area Transit Authority (DATA)
111 Vivian Street
Durham 27702–1612
Call 683-DATA for routes and schedules.
TTU information: 683–9657

R & G Airport Shuttle
RDU International Airport
P. O. Box 80245
Raleigh 27623
Individuals: 840–0262; Groups: 847–2226.

Robinson's Shuttle
2524 Apex Highway
Durham
405–2411 or (800) 490–2411

Triangle Transit Authority (TTA)
50 Park Drive
Durham 27702
549–9999
Airport shuttle: 687–4800
www.tta.dst.nc.us

Chapel Hill

Activities, Attractions, and Museums

Ackland Art Museum
South Columbia Street at Franklin Street
Chapel Hill 27599-3400
966–5736
www.unc.edu/depts/ackland/index.html
10:00 A.M. to 5:00 P.M. Wednesday through Saturday;
1:00 to 5:00 P.M. Sunday; closed Monday, Tuesday, and
major holidays. Free admission.

Coker Arboretum
North Carolina Botanical Garden
CB 3375 Totten Center
Chapel Hill 27599-3375
962–0522
Free admission.

Dean E. Smith Center
UNC Skipper Bowles Drive
Chapel Hill 27514
962–2296
www.smithcenter.edu
8:00 A.M. to 5:00 P.M. Monday through Friday; closed on
state holidays and event days. Free admission to the center; admission fees for events.

Morehead Planetarium
250 East Franklin Street
Chapel Hill 27599-3480

962–1236
www.unc.edu/depts/mhplanet
12:30 to 5:00 P.M. and 7:00 to 9:45 P.M. Sunday through Friday; 10:00 A.M. to 5:00 P.M. and 7:00 to 9:45 P.M. Saturday; closed Monday evenings, Christmas Eve and Christmas Day.
Admission fee.

UNC Visitors' Center
West Lobby, Morehead Planetarium
250 East Franklin Street
Chapel Hill 27599-3475
962–1630
www.unc.edu/depts/visitor/index
10:00 A.M. to 5:00 P.M. Monday through Friday. Closed major holidays.

Hotel
Carolina Inn
211 Pittsboro Street
Chapel Hill 27516
933–2001
www.carolinainn.com

Transportation
Chapel Hill Transit
306 North Columbia Street
Chapel Hill 27516
Route and schedule information: 968–2769
www.ci.chapel-hill.nc.us/transit

Area Attractions
You may want information on these attractions, some of which are located outside Raleigh, Durham, and Chapel Hill.

Joel Lane House
Corner of St. Mary's and West Hargett Streets
Raleigh 27601
833–3431
March through mid-December: 10:00 A.M. to 2:00 P.M.
Tuesday through Friday; 1:00 to 4:00 P.M. first and third
Saturdays of each month. Other tours by appointment.
Closed mid-December through February 28.

North Carolina Museum of Art
2110 Blue Ridge Road
Raleigh 27607
838–6262
www.ncartmuseum.org
9:00 A.M. to 5:00 P.M. Tuesday through Saturday; 9:00
A.M. to 9:00 P.M. Friday; 11:00 A.M. to 6:00 P.M. Sunday.
Closed Monday. Daily guided tours at 1:30 P.M.

Raleigh Memorial Auditorium
1 East South Street
Raleigh 27601
831–6060
Box office open 9:00 A.M. to 5:00 P.M. Monday through
Friday.

Bennett Place State Historic Site
4409 Bennett Memorial Road
Durham 27705
383–4345
April 1 through October 31: 9:00 A.M. to 5:00 P.M. Monday through Saturday; 1:00 to 5:00 P.M. Sunday.
November 1 through March 31: 10:00 A.M. to 4:00 P.M.
Tuesday through Saturday; 1:00 to 4:00 P.M. Sunday.
Closed Monday.
Free admission.

Duke Homestead State Historic Site and Tobacco Museum

2828 Duke Homestead Road
Durham 27705
477–5498
April 1 through October 31: 9:00 A.M. to 5:00 P.M. Monday through Saturday; 1:00 to 5:00 P.M. Sunday.
November 1 through March 31: 10:00 A.M. to 4:00 P.M. Tuesday through Saturday; 1:00 to 4:00 P.M. Sunday.
Hours may vary; contact site manager for details.
Free admission.

West Point on the Eno

5101 North Roxboro Road
Durham
471–1623
Park gates are open year-round from 8:00 A.M. to dark. Historic buildings are open 1:00 to 5:00 P.M., Saturday and Sunday, March through December. Closed January and February, except by appointment. Free admission.

Historic Hillsborough

Contact the Chapel Hill/Orange County Visitors Bureau
501 West Franklin Street, Suite 104
Chapel Hill 27516
968–2060 or (888) 968–2060
www.chocvb.org

Appendix C: Great Tastes

Raleigh, Durham, Chapel Hill, and the surrounding communities have hundreds of restaurants offering a variety of cuisines and prices. Have fun and explore the many choices. The restaurants listed below are only a sampling of those available to you in the area.

Angus Barn

Highway 70 at Airport Road
Raleigh 27628
787–3505

If you want to eat at a popular local restaurant, this is the place to go and the place to go if you are really hungry. It is almost a given that you will not leave hungry, for the plates are heaped with food. Be sure to follow tradition and pick up an apple from the huge wooden apple bins on your way out. Offering steaks as well as seafood, the Angus Barn serves dinner nightly. Reservations are accepted except on Saturday.

Char-Grill

618 Hillsborough Street
Raleigh 27602
821–7636

Walk up to the window, pick up a pencil and an order form, fill it out, and slide it through the slot. Then wait for a delicious hamburger. Chances are you will be waiting with others. There is no dining room at the Char-Grill; instead, folks regularly double up at one of the two outside picnic tables. The Char-Grill is popular with local business and government employees, many of whom pick up orders to take back to work.

Cooper's Barbecue

109 East Davie Street
Raleigh 27602
832–7614

A Southern barbecue platter is not complete without chopped or sliced pork with a clear sauce of vinegar, salt, and pepper, accompanied by coleslaw and hushpuppies. Cooper's Barbecue serves its barbeque North Carolina style.

42nd Street Oyster Bar

508 West Jones Street
Raleigh 27611
831–2811

First established in 1931, this restaurant offers crab cakes, clam chowder, and, of course, oysters. A spacious 1931 warehouse with art deco restoration adds to the appeal. Open for lunch and dinner daily and weekends for dinner only.

Greenshields Brewery & Pub

214 East Martin Street, City Market
Raleigh 27601
829–0214

Sample the beer and examine the brewing process while enjoying traditional English and popular American meals. The pub serves lunch and dinner daily.

Nana's Restaurant

2514 University Drive
Durham 27707
493–8545

Traditional Southern foods, such as sweet potatoes, bacon, and onions receive French and Italian accents, making them memorable dishes. Dinner is served Monday through Saturday; reservations recommended.

Pyewacket Restaurant
431 West Franklin Street
Chapel Hill 27516
929–0297
www.citysearch.com/rdu/pyewacket
Pyewacket offers an eclectic menu with Mediterranean and Southwest influences. Dine on the veranda or in the greenhouse overlooking an attractive courtyard. Lunch and dinner are served Monday through Thursday. Dinner is served on Friday through Sunday.

Appendix D: Useful Phone Numbers

Raleigh

Raleigh Police
Emergency, 911
Nonemergencies, 831–6311

Wake County Sheriff
Emergency 911
Nonemergency assistance, 856–6900
Fire emergency, 911

Hospitals
Raleigh Community Hospital, 954–3000
Wake Medical Center, 250–8000

Wake County Public Library
856–6710

Newspaper
The News & Observer, 829–4520

Poison Control
848–6946

Post Office
Main office, 420–5333

Road and Weather Conditions: Raleigh and Durham
Citizens Emergency Center Travel Advisory, 647–5225

State Highway Patrol: Raleigh and Durham
733–3861

Western Union: Raleigh and Durham
(800) 325–6000

Durham

Durham Police
Emergency, 911
Nonemergencies, 560–4427

Durham County Sheriff
Emergency, 911
Nonemergency assistance, 684–2444
Fire emergency, 911

Hospitals
Duke University Medical Center, 684–8111
Durham Regional Hospital, 470–4000

Durham County Library
560–0100

Newspaper
The Herald-Sun, 419–6500

Poison Control Center
(800) 848–6946

Post Office
Main office, 693–1976

Appendix E: Read All About It

Want to learn more about Raleigh, Durham, Chapel Hill, and the Triangle? The following books are a sample of the many you might enjoy.

Nonfiction

Anderson, Jean Bradley. *A History of Durham County, North Carolina.* Durham: Duke University Press, 1990.

If you love history, you will enjoy Anderson's detailed, comprehensive history of the area.

King, William E. *If Gargoyles Could Talk: Sketches of Duke University.* Durham: Carolina Academic Press, 1997.

Lefler, Hugh Talmage, ed. *North Carolina History: Told by Contemporaries.*

4th ed. Chapel Hill: The University of North Carolina Press, 1965.

Compiled and edited accounts of North Carolina political, social, and economic events, beginning with colonial North Carolina.

Lefler, Hugh T. and William S. Powell. *Colonial North Carolina: A History.* New York: Charles Scribner's Sons, 1973.

History of the state from the first explorations to the point where the state gained independence and statehood.

Perkins, David, ed. Raleigh: *A Living History of North Carolina's Capital.* Winston-Salem, N.C.: John F. Blair, 1994.

Chronologically arranged, this book contains pictures as well as accounts of much of Raleigh's history from the perspectives of journalists and reporters for the Raleigh *News & Observer.* The book also uses photos, letters, diaries, and oral histories, many of which are collected in *The News & Observer* files as well as state archives.

Raleigh for the People. Raleigh: Capital Broadcasting Company, Inc.

This is a beautiful photographic essay of the city of Raleigh. Full-color pictures depict political, social, and cultural life in the city.

Schumann, Marguerite E. *The First State University: A Walking Guide.* Chapel Hill: The University of North Carolina Press, 1972.

This pocket book divides the campus into walks and provides descriptions of buildings on the walk as well as colorful, entertaining anecdotes about people and things that call themselves Tar Heels.

Schumann, Marguerite E. *Strolling at State.* Raleigh, N.C.: State University Alumni Association, 1973.

This small pocketbook divides the campus into walks and provides descriptions of buildings on the walk, as well as colorful anecdotes about the university, its students, and its faculty.

Waugh, Elizabeth Culbertson, et. al. *North Carolina's Capital, Raleigh.* Chapel Hill: The University of North Carolina Press, 1967.

Published at the time of the city's 175th anniversary, this is an enjoyable account of Raleigh during the period 1760 to 1967. It includes photographs of many of Raleigh's historical buildings and houses accompanied by detailed and often anecdotal stories that offer the backgrounds of some of these buildings.

Fiction

Parker, Gwendolyn M. *These Same Long Bones.* Boston: Houghton Mifflin, 1994.

Set in the colorful Hay-Ti section of Durham, this novel provides a glimpse of life in a close-knit African-American community.

Patterson, James. *Kiss the Girls.* Boston: Little, Brown, 1995.

A beautiful Chapel Hill medical intern suddenly disappears and at almost the same time a Los Angeles reporter is killed. Washington, D.C.'s Alex Cross learns that two serial killers are competing against each other coast to coast.

Price, Reynolds. *Blue Calhoun.* New York: Atheneum, 1992.

Bluford "Blue" Calhoun, an ex-alcoholic music salesman living in Raleigh, North Carolina, in the 1950s is finally happy with his life and family, when a young girl walks into his life.

Poetry

Applewhite, James. *River Writing: An Eno Journal.* Princeton Series of Contemporary Poets. Princeton: Princeton University Press, 1990.

A collection of poems that form a journal of the poet's intimate encounters with nature and the Eno River.

Video

Shelton, Ron. *Bull Durham.* Image Entertainment. Directed by Ron Shelton, 1988.

A film about a North Carolina minor league baseball team and a groupie, starring Kevin Costner and Susan Sarandon. Set in the original Durham Bulls stadium.

Appendix F: Local Walking Clubs

Tarheel State Walkers Volkssport Club

402 Ryder Avenue
Landis 28088

Triangle Trailblazers

P.O. Box 90591
Raleigh 27675-0591

The Triangle Trailblazers and the Tarheel State Walkers Volkssport Club are both part of the American Volkssport Association, a network of clubs that sponsor noncompetitive walking, swimming, and biking events.

To receive a free general information packet that explains volkssporting and the American Volkssport Association, call the AVA (800–830–WALK) and leave your name, address, and phone number.

The AVA office can also give you the local phone contact for the AVA club mentioned above. This club sponsors several walking events in the Triangle area. The groups are also working on a Mountains to the Sea Year Round Walk in North Carolina. The AVA has information about where you can pick up descriptions of these walks.

Three shopping malls in the area offer mall walking. You will enjoy walking in the shelter of a mall when the weather is wet or cold or when you want to combine some window shopping with your walking.

Crabtree Valley Mall

Glenwood Avenue at I–440
Raleigh 27612
(800) 963–SHOP
www.crabtree-valley-mall.com

Cosponsored by Rex Healthcare, the Crabtree Walkers' Club currently has about 800 registered members. Rex

Healthcare provides the group with a speaker from various areas of the healthcare profession once a month.

Meetings are held the third Thursday of each month. Monthly breakfast meetings, a mileage record chart, and other incentives are provided by the club. To become a member of the Crabtree Walkers Club, register at Guest Services in the mall; however, you do not have to become a member in order to walk in the mall.

Two laps around one level of the center of the mall equal 1 mile. You are encouraged to walk from 5:00 to 10:00 A.M. on the lower mall level; 7:00 to 10:00 A.M. on the upper level, Monday through Saturday, and 8:00 A.M. to 1:00 P.M. on Sunday.

Northgate Mall

1058 West Club Boulevard
Durham 27705
I–176A from I–85
286–4400

This mall has no organized walking group; however, walkers are welcome to walk the 1-mile route around the mall. The mall opens at 6:30 A.M., and many walkers walk early before the stores open.

University Mall and Plaza

US 15501 at Estes Drive
Chapel Hill 27516
967–6934

Mall walkers are welcome at any time. The doors open at 7:00 A.M. on weekdays and Saturday for mall walkers; at 11:00 A.M. on Sunday.

Index

Meet the Author

Rebecca Mann enjoys walking and traveling—two hobbies that are combined in this book. She has co-authored a composition textbook with her husband, Pete, and has worked as a writing consultant for business and industry, in addition to her work as a college composition instructor. She and her family have traveled extensively in the United States, Canada, and Mexico, and she and her husband have led several tours to Europe.

Walking Raleigh/Durham combines her love for travel, history, North Carolina, and walking; she is enthusiastic about sharing this interest with others.

 A WHOLE DIFFERENT KIND OF WALK

Experience A Whole Different Kind of Walk

The American Volkssport Association, America's premier walking organization, provides noncompetitive sporting events for outdoor enthusiasts. More than 500 volkssport (translated "sport of the people") clubs sponsor walks in scenic and historic areas nationwide. Earn special awards for your participation.

For a free general information packet, including a listing of clubs in your state, call 1-800-830-WALK (1-800-830-9255).

American Volkssport Association is a nonprofit, tax-exempt, national organization dedicated to promoting the benefits of health and physical fitness for people of all ages.